I0427118

Journal of a Mental Patient

The Story of a Mind and Its Man

By

Michael Lee

ISBN: 1-4107-9286-2 (e-book)
ISBN: 1-4107-9285-4 (Paperback)

Library of Congress Control Number: 2003096701

This book is printed on acid free paper.

Printed in the United States of America
Bloomington, IN

1stBooks – rev. 10/13/03

Dedication

I hereby dedicate this book authoritatively, quantitatively, connotatively, relatively, completely, and seriously to those characters in my life mentioned, unmentioned, mimicked, copied, or invented throughout this book. For they are the ones – positive, negative, and neutral alike – who have saved me from myself, the world, and things unbeknownst to us all.

Acknowledgements

This section is a mixture of credit to those whom have helped me and is also the story of why and how I created this book. The people that will be listed below are not placed in any particular order except by paragraph size – largest to smallest – because it looks neat. Also, if I have forgotten to mention anyone, know now that if I've seen you, or talked to you at least once in life, I have not forgotten you, but either had nothing to say or couldn't remember your name. Furthermore, there are about a million more words that I could write about each subject and each person throughout this book and in this afterward. But, for the fact that they would have nothing to do with the plot, would be over-kill, wouldn't fit the character, would take several years to read/write, I've left them out, and will probably write them in future books.

I began writing in June of 2001 for fun and as a way of venting. I wrote the first entry (the only one that has not changed, save for spell-check), put it into my online diary, and then moved on to other things, not thinking that anything would come of it. Several people read it and liked it, so I began writing a continuous storyboard when I needed to vent and when I was feeling in an odd, mental patient type mood. Many people thought that it was a true story, failing to realize that mental hospitals don't have computers and most especially patients do not write on teen diary websites (this even after I mentioned the character's use of a typewriter). However, everyone seemed to like it nonetheless, so I continued to write entries. By the time I ran out of ideas for new entries, I had written twenty-five separate pieces. In my tenth grade English class, I jokingly said that I was going to write a book out of them. Later that day I copy-pasted all twenty-five of the entries into my word processor, and together had forty-four pages. Through the end of tenth grade and following summer on into the middle of eleventh grade I slaved over the computer for hours at a time, rewording, reorganizing, and adding on to those forty-four pages, until I had a novel of whatever size yours is now. For the most part, the stories and ideas displayed throughout the book, are pieces of events, ideas, and conversations that I have had in real life, with my real friends; I have made up very little. That is the story of this book. But now to the credits:

Brian and Andy are my two best friends in the world. I've known Brian since first grade and have spent a lot of time with him during school and at his homes. I thank Brian for always being creative and out-going, (I am the anal one) and for always going along with all of my asinine ideas about blowing stuff up and or going out for no reason. I also thank him for giving me the experience of having an overly depressed friend, so that I knew what to look for when I slowly declined to a similar level. Because of this, I was able to bring him back up (somewhat), and myself – I learn through example – and was able to portray that similar depression more realistically in my book. Andy is my Big Tall Korean Friend – I seriously call him that. He, being Asian, arrogant, and good at math, has been the one that has kept my ego from inflating bigger than it already is now. Although recently, we've not been able to talk on the phone, I do appreciate those four years of daily eight-hour conversations. It's odd, you would never think that he would have much more than a mechanical, mathematical brain, but when you really get to know him, you find that he is very intelligent and can in fact, write very well and with obvious emotion. He is developed my fun, outspoken sense of humor. I thank him for inspiring my sarcasm and satire. Both of them have encouraged me by through conversations, spending time with me, putting me down when needed, and by nourishing my ideas. Brian and Andy play the parts of Isaac and Frank, their personalities in this book are exact replicas.

Then there is Jeanelle, the strange girl that never stops changing on me. I met her in eighth grade during a field trip at the end of the year, and shortly after, she got my phone number. From that day, until I left with my dad that summer, the phone was constantly in use. At that time in my life, many things were going wrong and I lacked control, stability, and happiness. For the next three months, she helped me gain some of those things, or at least helped me to realize how to get those things on my own. It's difficult to put into words, but she has taught me the basics of everything that I know now about teenage life and survival. I still like to give several other people and myself credit; it's not fair to say she fixed me completely, because I don't think I realized what she was trying to say until later. Anyway though, she was the first person I let get close and was the first person I loved more than a friend but less than a lover. She taught me several other things as well, about relationships and the like, and one of those fine times just so happened to take place at Wet n' Wild...but I'm not allowed to discuss this event, so I will continue in another direction. After that summer, we drifted apart and she began to change again (she hates sameness), and for the longest time, I considered her dead to me. Many months passed, and only recently have things gotten better, for she is different, and so am I. However, we have both worked hard to bring things to antebellum; it has worked. Jeanelle plays the part of Jane in this book, her death represents our separation, and how I was forced to finally learn without her – she is still alive in real life and we are still in love.

Strangely, I met Rosie through Jeanelle over the phone during a conference call. After that, we talked on the phone and visited each other quite often. Rosie helped me in that, she opened my mind to different ways of self-expression, fun, and taught me about myself. Because of her, I changed a lot: dyed my hair, wore a dog collar with second-hand clothes, and wrote angst poetry. I did this for two years, but now have a job and do not dye my hair and my collar does not fit, but I still enjoy dressing in the same exact five outfits I've had for the last three years. However, because of this, I learned about people (good and bad) and finally formed my own opinions about the world, my own style, and about everything else related to the world and myself. Also, Rosie was very helpful in her blatant description and irritation at the annoying and rude little things that I did. She helped me to experience the life that exists inside my mind and I learned tact. Sadly, she quickly disappeared, got married, and moved away. However sad this was, I think that we both got from each other, or at least I got from her, what we needed and I will always remember her. Recently, we have started communicating again and I will soon be taking a road trip from Las Vegas, Nevada, to New Jersey, to go see her. That too is love.

Aaron is a male version of Rosie, and it's interesting and appreciated. I've known him since first grade, and we were enemies until seventh, and have only been good friends for the last three years. I don't know how Aaron grew up and I don't remember how we met, in fact, it's odd that we are such good friends because we are different in many ways, but seem to have commonalties in just the right places to make us good friends. Because of this, we both emphasize each other's better qualities, or make up for the other's inferior or non-existent ones. In fact, we've decided that if we were genetically mixed into one person, that that person would be perfect: insane strength and speed, all-knowing, magnanimous personality, large genitals, and tall dark n' handsome. Of course, since this is expensive, we only share a brain for the time being. Anyway, Aaron is like Rosie because he is very blatant, and rarely compliments people, so that when he does, you know that it means much more than he actually said. His knowledge of pretty much everything is extensive to the point of an arguable point for both sides of every story. Because of this, he has proved to be a great tool and friend, both in learning and in destruction (we blow things up a lot). I regret not mentioning Aaron's character more than a few times, but I plan to use him in future books because he is funny and adds an interesting edge to any story. Aaron plays the part of Jonathan mentioned in the beginning and is a main character in the prequel that I am currently writing.

Richard Benwal van Duevendyke, or Benwal for short. He is the Canadian man that I found myself obsessed with because of his prolific, spiteful writing. After leaving him many online diary notes that never seemed to have an ending, he e-mailed me and we are now online best friends. He is me in Canadian form, left-handed, grocery store worker and all. He has put into words (in this book even) some of the things that I have thought or said, but could not do justice on paper. For, he has a much more active voice than I do because I either forget my point for writing something, change my mind, or don't have an "in your face" attitude about it. However, I have the ongoing want, focus, and ideas to make an entire book out of it all. We have both helped each other mutually, through "listening" to each other's complaints, laughing about inane things, typing profound advice, and by sharing creepy-cool music. His writing has been a displayed in part of chapter ten;

he has played a large role in inspiration, it's what he does best, and not even on purpose.

And now I will thank my mom and Neil, for they have supported me financially and with encouragement, and one of them has been the spawn of this entire book, which has turned into much more than just the inane bitching about her. Without my mom, I would not have angst to write about being in a mental hospital – proverbial or real. It's hard to put into words anything about either of them because for the most part my mom is better now, I don't dwell on bad things, and I forgive easily, so I suppose what the book says will have to suffice. Just know that even though I'm unappreciative, I appreciate it all. I have good parents – which I've just now realized – and I couldn't wish for anyone different. They have taught me so many things about being a good person in this world that I don't even realize it until I see them doing the same things that I do, or visa versa. My stubborn morals, mannerisms (not manners, I'm terrible at the table), and attitudes are a direct product of their teachings. Together, they have turned me into a responsible, disciplined, intelligent, well-oiled machine that thinks for himself and is proud of too much.

Now, we come to my dad. He is one of the coolest people I know, and he loves cartoons. I love him unconditionally despite all the people that have tried to turn me against him. For, he is my dad and I couldn't care less what "horrible things" he's done in his past life, because he has shown me as much love as he possibly can. It's odd, many people spite their fathers when they leave, the only thing I did was understand why. Other people feel abandoned; I instead hear the music of the hold button and wait happily and patiently for him to return. My dad has shown me millions of things, good and bad, through example, by experience, and by driving me around the country in his semi-truck. I have learned so much from him that it makes school look like a motivational cassette tape, because I can at least use what I've learned from my dad to survive life and have fun – at the same time too! Thanks daddy, I love you man! My three parents of course played themselves. The death of my father represents the change he went through after being in jail, for he is now a different kind of teaching dad, but my dad nonetheless – he is always there for me, and I hope he understands that after reading this. I regret that he had to die here, but it is more extreme than I feel and it had to be done in order show the character's extreme emotional states.

In closing, I thank my teachers, assorted friends, family, girlfriends, acquaintances, and customers. I especially thank my English teachers because they are the ones that have made it possible for me to write a complete, proper sentence. I also thank all the teachers whom have ever gotten along with me and for teaching me their subjects about life. Without them, I would not know how people work, think, tolerate, survive, have fun, or live – among many other things – all at the same time. And without all of those people whom have inadvertently said something important, have made me think, have pissed me off, have made me happy, whom I have loved, whom I have tolerated, and whom I've seen in the halls only once, I would not be me. I thank these people as well, for they probably don't even know who they are, but they are important nonetheless.

In conclusion, as I end this longer than I had expected afterward, I say thank you one more time to everyone in the world for helping me find enlightenment (the cheese/the goal that our dear friend finally found but never identified). Finally, I say with final finality, that despite gender, personality, smell, amount of unshaven body hair, and annoying habits, I thank, appreciate, and love you all, for, as I've said before, you are the ones who have saved me, each other, yourselves, and the world from everything.

Introduction

What you are about to read is the collected journal entries of the most fictional character you will never meet. In reality, the characters of this novel are nothing more than a collection of my personality – if I had made certain said decisions in my life – mixed with that of my friends' personalities and then stirred together with a bit of imagination and poetic license.

I tell you now that everything that happens, every made-up word, coincidence, contradiction, nuance, nook, and cranny of this book is done on purpose and for a purpose. It may however, be difficult to find and or understand that purpose, but if you do find it, more power to you. In fact, *all* power to you, for you are a genius in the true sense of the word, and you should spread the news of your findings to everyone you know. Or, if you are not such the sociable person, you should write a letter telling me what *you* think, for I am always interested in feedback whether it is positive or negative.

For the fact that this book is filled with much philosophy and probably a lot of symbolism, it should be analyzed in a way that would make only your past, present, or future high school English teacher proud. Of course, if you dislike symbolism or your English teacher, just enjoy reading the book for the entertainment value of the story and take it literally. This book is much like the Bible in that it can be read both ways and enjoys telling you how to live your life in an abstract manner; so like I've said many times in my life, enjoy!

Finally, I leave you, the reader, with a small but necessary warning. I pride myself in the ability to "get into peoples' heads." So, if you find yourself going perhaps a bit crazy, take a break to sort out your thoughts, breathe, and analyze yourself, then pick up the book and press on. If, for some reason, you do not find your head being, "gotten into," perhaps you're too strong a person, or you just aren't reading deep enough into the words and should try harder...Either way I wish you luck. Good life, good day, good reading, good thoughts, and good karma, for these things will save us all...

Prologue

Suddenly, a car speeds across Main Street during the Independence Day Parade and hundreds of papers come flying out of it. Seeing this, a stout, chubby, balding man picks one up and reads it passively. He pauses for a moment to look up in thought, then as sudden and as quick as the car sped by, he begins to collect all the pages, as if it is his new life goal. After picking some from the air, the ground, off of people, out of hands, and following one float all the way to its warehouse to pick a paper from it, he is satisfied that he has every page and immediately heads home.

After several hours of arduously reassembling the pages into chronological order, he sits back in his chair in awe and with relief of his seemingly pointless task – though he'd argue that it was everything but –, picks up the pages, and begins to read...

Part 1

1
And It Starts

I feel less fearful of the world today.

But that is only because my doctor says I am doing better. Dr. Shutz thinks that I should write a journal to try to get my feelings out onto paper so that I can learn to identify and control my emotions. He says that I should only write positive things if I can, but if not, I should sort out my bad feelings rationally and with good explanations. Only then will I be on the road to recovery...heh...recovery...

Personally, I'm not sure if I feel better, but I have been acting and thinking a bit differently, so I suppose *something* is working. I slept in my bed last night, it's cozy, now I know what I've been missing each night on that cold concrete floor. The bed was nice, but it was too nice for me, I think I will sleep on the floor again tonight.

Something interesting happened to me today, Malcolm, the man who thinks he is Ted Bundy, found a piece of paper somewhere, folded it into a shape with a point and attempted

4

to murder me with it. I was only slightly amused, but the two orderlies stopped him so I returned to my corner and my dry state of mind. I like it there, it brings me comfort, and it is a much easier reality to face than the reality that exists outside of these walls.

It's funny, my family thinks I am insane, that's why I'm here, personally I think I'm fine, I just need my own time and space. But, that's ok I guess, I was endangering the family and that's not good, therefore I accept my place here. Besides, I have many friends, mostly Doctor Shutz, he's a nice man, very old, wise, and he always has something encouraging to say. I like his office, it's very cluttered and filled with paintings and drawings made by his kids instead of organized and plain with several diplomas displayed here and there like some doctors' offices are.

Dr. Shutz is a good doctor because of his empathy; I have great respect for that ability and wish that I could understand people the way that he does. Empathy is especially helpful in his school of therapy – Humanistic – because it focuses on the unfaltering positive reinforcement of its patients and their ideas. In fact, accordingly to a book I once read on the schools of psychology, many Humanistic psychiatrists need therapy themselves; I find that ironic in a morbid sort of way. Seemingly though, Dr. Shutz is good enough at his job that it's rumored that he has in fact, "cured" people before.

It's nice to see people being "cured" and I only wish them the best. I was once asked if I thought everyone had hope, I said yes...but did not count myself as everyone, for I am hopeless. I've been in this place for three years, it is my home, and I never expect to leave. However, Doctor Shutz seems to think differently, he has me on a new drug, he had them color it orange just for me, isn't he nice? Anyway, he thinks that this one may do the trick, and if it means that I will not experience a full range of emotions, that's fine with me. For, it is much easier to be a zombie than it is to have many violent thoughts and tendencies along with uncontrollable urges and moods. It is an extremely difficult mind to live with; you have no idea how much it upsets the people that you love. But for now I will just see what happens, play it by ear I suppose, but I shouldn't get my hopes up, treatments rarely work and "cures" do not exist.

Facing Fear

I start to walk,
I hear a noise
I Stop.
Silence –
I Start again,
I see a shadow
I turn around
Nothing is there
I continue
I suddenly turn around!
I see him!
Fear!
He stalks me!
I look into his eyes and laugh –
He looks into my eyes and laughs –
I am confused
He takes a step forward,
I disappear
Fear has won again

4/29/10

Today I was an observer.

Normally I do not notice my surroundings all too well, but with my new found treatments I've decided to take advantage of my ability to notice insignificant details. So I sat in my corner of the room and noticed the characters of my game.

One drab individual paced through the ward nervously, almost as if he was waiting for something. I, for a moment, wondered what this poor man could have been waiting for, and for how long. Sadly though, he became tiresome to me because he did not answer my questions, and I diverted my eyes to another lonely soul.

This one seemed strangely calm in the creepiest way possible, so I found him more interesting than the first. Watching his eyes was like watching a child's bouncy-ball and equally as entertaining. His body language suggested that he had some sort of purpose and that no one could interrupt his task. As I looked closer, I also noticed the rapid movement of his lips and the twitching of his fingers; they were not sporadic, but rhythmic and controlled. It's unfortunate that he is stuck in here, unable to complete his seemingly important task...perhaps he was to save the world from itself? Oh well.

I continued sitting in my spot for several more hours and much to my surprise, I began to see a pattern among the movement of people. Almost every "group" had its own distinctive cadence. The OCD patients seemed to be making the biggest contribution to this pattern with their constant rhythms and obsessive movements. Those with anxiety disorders created an almost maddening rhythm with their incessant twitching and mumbling – luckily, I've learned to ignore such things over time. Some of the others seemed to be circling, talking, and thinking for no reason and to no one. At the moment, it is a bit more difficult for me to remember specific instances, but I'm sure that in this new journal there will be plenty of space for specifics.

Other than that though, my day was filled with nothing but constant inconsequential thoughts and actions as it normally is. Actually, that's not true, for lunch we had tuna sandwiches – my favorite. BUT! Such is the life of me. I'm tired though, I will retire to my floor to write again another day.

4/30

I watched TV today – not good.

I usually hate watching TV because of the violence and inane lies that it spews. I figure, if I want my daily dose of violence, lies, sex, and or other expletives, I'll just read the Bible, but today I felt compelled to see what was going on in the world.

As I walked through the hall, I passed by the Game Room and saw something rather interesting on the news, so I stopped to watch. It turns out that the car companies have all finally decided to join together to make one "Super Car." It supposedly will be one hundred percent electric (no need for fossil fuels of any kinds), is made of super-light-weight materials (it will only weigh about nine hundred pounds), and it is almost fully automated, save for emergency situations.

This is funny to me because nearly eight years ago I remember them talking about the same car and how expensive and impossible to mass-produce them it would be. It seems that all it takes to get something done is people joining together and agreeing on one cause. I wonder on how many other things that would work with, never on anything else I'm sure – HA!

If only these stupid humans would figure out that if they worked *together*, more things would get accomplished and on a more regular basis! I mean look at all of the wars we've had over the entire existence of the world; not to mention the one's we have had recently! They think *I* should be locked up? What kind of crap is that!? If anything, the rest of the world should be the one in mental institutions, NOT ME! I swear to God, when I get out of here I'm going to teach these people a thing or two about keeping themselves in control! STUPID ASS…

…I'm gonna go before I rant more about how the world screws us all over –

On second thought, I think I'm ok, so nevermind. Anyway, as I was saying, TV is the spawn of all evil and I think that we should abolish it at once. I only say this because there's so much violence and horribleness in the world that we don't need the TV promoting it and showing us how to kill, lie, or steal better than we all already do.

The news is one of the worst too; they show every single bad thing that they can possibly find before they show anything even remotely good. It's like they're trying to kill the spirits of every single individual in this world by leaving us sad and depressed, but then finally boost our spirits in the slightest at the end of the show.

Then, to make matters worse, the actual shows themselves are becoming more unrealistic than reality! What with all these "Reality TV" shows and all; the point of them is to stick some said number of people in the most dangerous situation possible and then see if they survive. Why, just yesterday, Barney was telling me about one of them; they stuck some person in an alligator infested swamp, so that he could swim to the bottom of the swamp, grab some orange flag, then come back up without getting his ass bit off. And for what, one million dollars!? What's the point of that? Most of that money will be given to the government for taxes anyway! Oi, it's so dumb…what's next, people chasing each other through the country trying to KILL each other off for one million dollars!? No. I refuse to take part in any of this mayhem; it's simply ridiculous.

AND! If that's not bad enough, you should see the drama shows they have now. The last show that attempted to have good moral values lost its sponsors and ratings for the sole reason that there "weren't enough explosions." I can't believe that that has actually become one of the only reasons for keeping a show on TV, for the amount of explosions! Not to mention the crude nudity and sex that's been sneaking by unnoticed by the masses! That makes me want to cry! But then again so does the rest of the world, but that's another story for another time. I'm just hoping that there are at least a few other people in the world that will stand up against TV with me, not that it'll make a difference, but still it's fun to dream.

Possessive TV

He's evil
He's mean
And very addictive,
He sucks you in
With lights and sounds
Then spits you out when you're "gone"

Because you sit there and watch
You eat and you laugh
You lose the IQ you had to start
You begin to get fat
With your damned Yankees hat,
And right when you are
About to snap,
A commercial comes on
Look! only $9.99
Oh no!
Oh dear!
It almost got me!
I will not
Can not
Let it get me
So what do I do?
I hear you ask

I refuse to watch
Because the evil within
The possessive TV

Anyway, enough of my bitching, I think I'll go to bed, even though it's only seven o'clock – there's nothing else to do. So! I'm out...

5/1

Today it got hotter.

It's late at night and I'm sweating because of the humidity. It's rather disgusting to say the least. I do not enjoy body fluids especially the ones that smell bad, but I suppose it doesn't matter, for it's late and I have no one to impress. In fact, it seems that I no longer have anyone to impress at all, most of which myself. I used to pride myself in my "presentability," but recently I'm lucky if I'm even shaven. I rarely take a shower, and when I do, it's short and not so relaxing, for it is difficult for me to take a shower with other men – rather disgusting too. However, right now I wouldn't mind it too much, because my body is wet to the touch and obscenely squishy. I seriously do hope that this humidity passes because I'd much rather be hot and dry than hot and wet – I'm not at a water park for God's sake! Oh well, I'll deal with it.

Today is Sunday so I decided to give religion a try again – it didn't work. Besides the fact that not many people showed up – mostly because they cannot sit still for such a long time and because they blame God for their problems (if they can think well enough to do so). It was entertaining to say the least, for I no longer put much stock into religion in general. It's not that I don't like God, sure He's a great guy, I just don't like the way He goes about doing certain things like, umm, getting followers perhaps? I find it annoying, but will not go into right now because I'm having a little bit more trouble thinking than I usually do. Perhaps another time, after I've thought it out more thoroughly, I will go into my logical conclusions on religion more in-depth.

Speaking of which, accordingly another religious group that call themselves the, "People for a Better Way of Life," have decided to start little military skirmishes with Eurasian countries that do not have a monotheistic religion. Reason eighty-four why I don't like religion, stupid people trying to fix other stupid people in the interest of sending them to this so-called Heaven. What about all the people in Asia? How come they never found Jesus? That's trillions of people over the course of the world that have died and gone to Hell by *default*! I find that a bit unfair don't you God? Oh well, sucks for them, I happen to like Asian religions better anyway, less emphasis on following so many contradictory rules and more emphasis on inner peace and getting along with each other. I mean, you never see any Buddhists killing Muslims and whatever not, do you? NO! Exactly why white people are stupid, end of story. ☺ But seriously, it's quite asinine what they do; I don't like it at all.

But then again, I never was one for sheep, not too tasty, not too smart, and too hairy – just like people. I don't trust them much; most people are so obsessive about the wrong things that they'd be more inclined to kill you for a nickel then they would to help out. I suppose that's a bit unfair, but I am only generalizing, so that makes it ok. Anyway, being in here is probably better anyway, I'm protected from stress, judgement, lies, some stupidity, and from interruptions. It's rather tranquil in its own creepy, you're-in-an-insane-asylum-with-a-bunch-of-people-that-could-kill-you-and-will-never-know-that-there's-anything-wrong-with-them-so-long-as-they're-on-thorazeen-24/7, sort of way. So in hindsight, I hate it, but will live a prosperous life full of loathing and self-doubt that will end with me wondering, "what *could* I have done with my life?" But until the end, I suppose I will shoot for the first two.

Anyway, I think I'm finally falling asleep in this horrible humid heat of beginning summertime and so I will fall asleep in a puddle of my own sweat, only to wake up disgusted, smelly, sticky, and grouchy – what a wonderful day tomorrow will be. – Bad night!

5/2

I feel more fearful of the world today.

This time it doesn't have anything to do with my mood, luckily. No, instead it has something to do with what I was thinking about...the outside world. For the last few years a lot of things have fallen into social decline; the economy, government, foreign relations, and pretty much everything else that one could possibly think of. So, the reason I say that I feel more fearful of the world today is because, it has become a scary place to live in. If I had kids I would think twice about bringing them up in any major or small cities, and instead would move to the sticks (Kentucky or Iowa) or what's left of it. For, if you live in a city nowadays, it seems that the cost of living has gotten so high that only the rich and famous can live in apartments. In fact, accordingly to one of the new night-shift guys, Duncan, his last job paid eight-fifty an hour for minimum wage! My first job only paid five ninety-five an hour, and that was only about four years ago! I think we call that mass inflation but it could be just supply and demand, either way it's rather disturbing that companies pay that much for good workers, or that people demand that much to survive – either way no one wins the deal, except the church because they're tax exempt.

Money isn't the only thing being affected though, the military, technology and military technology have taken a turn for the better, but with better technology comes greater responsibility and greater risk of mass destruction. I've heard something about the near completion/perfection of anti-matter energy. In high school physics we talked about the mixture of neutrally charged energy, mixing with positively charged energy (that starts out as matter). When those two things mix, not much happens until you do something to them (I think it was super-heat, suddenly shift the charge or expose them to some kind of energy frequency, it was still unknown at the time) and suddenly you have a massive cascade reaction that results in more than nuclear proportions. This is a wonderful power source when contained; it's cleaner, but more expensive to use for power because of all of the control equipment involved. However, when this crap is let into the hands of people who don't care about power, it is, can be, and has been used for massive destruction! I mean, it's not really *that* big of a deal that the stuff is unstable when not controlled unless you had a fondness for the entire north, east, south, and semi-central sides of Paris.

Anyway, we're just lucky that it's hard to find and make this stuff and that none of the remaining terrorist factions (the ones that we attempted to destroy in the "War on Terror" but didn't) have it yet, or we'd all be in a butt-load of trouble. How we soon forget that only a year ago...wow, two years ago, a large band of terrorists mangled Washington D.C. with their/our kamikaze airliners filled with some nuclear power isotopes.

Well I'm done ranting because I forgot what my point was, so I'm going to go get some food because I'm hungry. I think today is egg salad with baked beans and something only resembling a slice of ham that *I* think is really a lily pad with color additive. Slow day.

5/5 11:47 a.m.

I just had a dream.

It's about 3:43 A.M. right now and I just had a funny dream that I *have* to write about!

Ok, so I'm in a large room that resembles that of the dinning room in my old house. There is something between me and someone else, like a table or some kind of furniture. The walls are lined with shelves that are holding tons of expensive glass and pottery stuff; china plates, glass sculpture statue thingees, little miniature kitties, and a lot of crystal glasses and other various objects that break. I personally like breaking things and definitely get a kick out of the way things are shattered, so if I were ever in a position like this in real life, I would probably take advantage of it in the same way that I did in the dream. We – not sure who the other person was – both have the aforementioned things on our shelves. I know this because I remember looking back to find something and saw that I had just as many breakables as the other person did.

Anyway, we start by throwing rocks, and just nicking and knocking over things. Then it gets a little bit more intense and all of a sudden, things are shattering. We throw a few of the plates randomly and scowl and laugh at each other at the same time, seemingly it's all fun and games. All of a sudden though, things are crashing all over the place (I've got to admit, it's rather fun to watch glass explode), then somehow the other person finds a large pottery bowl and takes out an entire shelf of my stuff. But then! I get one of my massive pottery pieces and lay waste to their china plates!! MwuAHAhaA!! She then finds metal spoons (don't ask how they came in I don't know) and breaks the window to the door I just remembered I was hiding behind (with another person actually...hmmm I never saw their faces and only had a slight feeling of who they were). Next, I find this really neat-o looking gold, Indian plate, and throw it like a Frisbee, totally wiping out an entire shelf of expensive looking crystal glasses! IT WAS SO COOL! It went *crash, crackle, crunch*!! But then some funny looking cop walked in, so we decided to stop…oh well, it was pretty funny, I looked at the floor and it was covered with magical glass shards and crap like that. At the end of the dream everyone hugged and or shook hands and made up and it was like there was no animosity between any of us at all – how strange.

I just wanted to write about that dream because I found it more amusing than anything I've seen or heard in a long time, and this will prove to be an uplifting entry among none. But it's pretty late right now…or early depending on how you look at it, so I will return to sleep – night

I feel very evil today.

I'm not sure why, it might have something to do with the fact that my mom came to visit unexpectedly. I hate her with a cold dark passion befitting that of the devil, I truly do; she's the reason I'm in here. Well, more or less, I could have stopped myself, I have the self-control, but I really didn't care at that point. I was sick of her and her irrational behavior. I won't get into it now because it upsets me to talk about it, perhaps another time. But let's just say I did something very bad, and instead of going to Juvenile Detention, I got sent here instead. Oh well, shit happens what can I do. Even Dr. Shutz was disappointed about my mom's surprise visit, I heard him telling her how much progress I was making, but that today I was acting as if I had made absolutely no progress at all. I don't really think she was mad like she normally is, but I could be wrong, I was too busy humming and rocking to really notice much of anything. Luckily though, she finally caught on to my discontent – to say the least – and left because she "cares."

However, I doubt that she cares or ever really did or will care too extremely much, because at least then she would never have driven me to this state of mind. I sit here daily, in my designated corner, loathing the world, myself, and most of all, her. It's not always healthy but it's what I know best, so I really don't do much to change it despite Dr. Shutz's disapproval of this type of thinking/behavior. I know I probably *should* change, but change is too difficult – even though I've not quite tried it – so I won't. Besides, even if I finally did change, what would that mean for me? I'd always have the lingering memories of what I used to be and the reasons that I used to be this way, so what's there to stop me from having problems in the future? I don't know either.

Well, Dr. Shutz says that if I did cope with my problems, that the memories would serve as reminders of what I *used* to be and could perhaps help me to learn; either way they would not cause regression. I personally do not know, but am willing to try anything – to an extent – but am deathly afraid of what could happen. I don't know, perhaps I'm just lacking motivation of the sorts, or maybe I'm procrastinating, but like I've said before, I do not usually consider myself someone that is "curable."…I guess I could always give it a try, but for what? I have no idea…maybe something will come up soon and jolt my interests in change, but then again maybe not. I guess we'll have to see…

5/8

Today was nostalgic.

I found myself missing my friends today because it has been so long since they last visited. I wonder if they even live in town anymore. It's not really *too* interesting of a place to live, but it definitely keeps its inhabitants happy. We all grew up here; Isaac, Frank, Jane, Leslie, and Dick, we all went to the same schools and we all hung-out together whenever possible. It's a great existence, being best friends I mean, without them I probably would have been here earlier and in worse shape too, so from that perspective I suppose I'm a lucky person.

Isaac, Frank, and Jane are my BEST friends in the whole world! We used to plan on us all living together in one small apartment. Heh, because of our cheapness, we planned on only having two beds and every night we would rotate sleeping places, two of us on a bed, then one of us on the couch and the other in the bathtub. Of course, the rotation would be altered if any of us had brought home a guy or girl. That person would get the bed for the night. Anyway, I planned on going to college to become a psychologist (funny how things work out), Frank planned on going to MIT to get his Robotic Technologies degree, Jane wanted to be a child psychologist, and Isaac just kind of floats along as a vagabond. It looks like my part of the idea didn't really work out...I wonder how theirs went...

Jane especially though, is my best friend of all time, not because she is better than the guys are, but because she could provide certain attentions that the guys couldn't provide (not that I'd want them to provide those *certain* attentions). She was more though, she was the only one that believed I could, can, and will make it through life with a wonderful success story to tell at the end.

I have good friends though, because, at first, they came to see me all the time, I loved it, they made me feel a lot better, like nothing was wrong at all. At that time, I was much more open and extroverted, so we all spent a lot of time watching TV (ack!), playing games, talking outside, and meeting new people. They all kept me informed of their life's progress and I kept them informed of my progress as well. Their lives were usually a lot more interesting though, but they listened to me nonetheless. They all graduated from high school a year later (when I'd be graduating too). Isaac and Frank ended up living together after all (like we had all planned), but Jane went her separate way and moved to an apartment downtown so that she could be closer to "her people." She enjoys being around grief-stricken people because she's constantly analyzing and experimenting on them with or without their knowledge. In fact, I believe that at one point, I was one of her experiments, so now she knows me much better than she should and sometimes uses it against me. Meanwhile though, I sit in here with my life on hold, waiting for some new drug or therapy technique to save me so that I can go back to my friends and my old life.

Soon after the end of high school, my friends' visits became fewer and farther between. The group, however, didn't give up on me for a long time and for that I love them...only recently did they stop coming. Well...if you consider a year ago recent...I suppose no one really comes to visit me anymore.

I remember my eighteenth birthday party – over a year ago – everyone was there, Jane, Isaac, Frank, Leslie, Dick, Tony, and some other friends and family members. The Ward Master gave us a small room for a party. At that time, I had only been in here for about a year or more, and things were looking good, well, not really come to think of it, that was actually one of my hardest times.

But now, nearly two years later, no one really ever comes at all, it's sad, but I get over it, I always do, and besides, I think I would have given up on myself after two years too, so I don't hold it against them. If I could, I would try to call them, but it's not as if I've ever seen a phone in this place. Besides, I doubt they still live in the same places they used to live, with their parents, and I never got any new phone numbers, so nevermind.

Well I suppose it's not true that NO ONE ever visits, I mean, my mom just came the other day, despite her visits ill effects on me...Oh well, maybe one of these days I'll see them all again...or not. But enough of that, I think maybe I'll take a nap. Good day.

5/10 4:36 p.m.

Michael Lee

Today is good.

They let me have my Music Pad back today, so I played a very nice piece of music using the organ setting. If I could get a hold of some staff paper I would write this stuff down so that I could copyright it and make some money off of my music instead of letting it fall upon deaf ears. Oh well, maybe one of these days I will. It's sort of a waste – my five years of band – because I could seriously have made a career out of my musical talents. But I suppose that that ship has sailed, and that there is probably no real productive reason to dwell upon my would-be ideas.

Anyway, I think I was feeling intelligent today too, because I wrote some poetry and put it up on the wall with the other two hundred eleven poems – all of varying degree of quality and deepness. One of these days I'm going to put them into a book called, "The Collected Works of a Struggling Soul." I mean, it would probably be a book worth reading if you were interested in that sort of thing. It would show the thought processes of my mind through hundreds of different life experiences and emotions. Anyone that, at one time or another, needed/needs help in their life on how to sort something out, would probably benefit from what I have to say. At the very least, it would definitely make for interesting poetry reading. Accordingly to friends, teachers, and strangers alike, my poems are very well written because they are deep, easy to understand, and make you think. Not to mention I have semi-good format, style, ideas, voice, and whatever else you might need to make a good poem. I suppose it helps that I took a Poetry class way back in the day and got my Poetry Laureate Degree from some online poetry place. But until I actually make these into a book, I'll just keep writing and wallpapering.

I enjoy writing though, it makes me feel in touch with myself, and that is ALWAYS a good thing. (*He takes a look at several of His wallpaper-poems and reads one aloud:*

"Immortality

I live forever!
I am immortal!
I see the world
From objective eyes
I've seen it all and done it twice
But some things never change

For the wars of the world
Do never end
Death and destruction
Is the way of life
It's no more different
Than the animal kingdom
Only we are more intelligent

Or are we?
I ask this question
Because I do not know
Of all the time
I've roamed this earth
I haven't seen much proof at all
For the humans think, they are superior
When all they do, is fight and quarrel
They have no peace
Nor peace of mind,
But they still try
And will die trying —

For I foresee
The end of the world,
Not the place in which we live
But in the place in which we think
For the mind of humans
Is slowly changing
For the better,
For the worse,
I do not know
But I do know one thing — it's for sure
I will be the last to go." He holds the poem, looks up to ponder
its meaning, then returns to writing in His journal.)

...Heh, my obsession with being immortal...

After closer inspection though, I've found that many of my pieces resemble each other in many ways, I'm basically repeating myself with different words that are in a different order. A lot of them have to do with either, being angry, hurting someone, loving someone, or about society and it's odd nuances. Most of my experiences seem to involve avoiding people and or missing out on something, and the few times that it's not about those things, seem only mildly interesting...

Eh, I don't even know why I continue sometimes. I guess so long as they're not exactly the same, the stupid sheep of this world won't notice that every poem in any book that I might write, is basically the same - I guess that's called theme! I'm sorry, Dr. Shutz says I shouldn't think like that because it means that I'm not making progress. Oh well, I don't know how to erase with this typewriter so I'll continue and hope that he doesn't see this page.

Anyway, what else happened today...Oh yeah! I went outside! I'm very proud of myself! The early summer sun was very soothing and it made me feel like a young kid again. It reminded me of when I used to walk outside after a long day of reading in my freezing house, only to be warmed to the bone by the bright sun. It took a very long time for my eyes to adjust to the brightness today, but that's ok, I was in no hurry to do anything else and did not mind the blinding wait. It was a nice day, I don't think I've ever realized it, but this place has a very large front courtyard. I mean, you'd think I would have noticed that after about four years, but I guess I never got around to checking it out. I decided to take advantage of my "outsideness" and explored.

It seems that the building is five stories high and fairly large in square footage. The entire building seemed like that of an ancient Victorian Home but I doubt that the place is really that old. Its perimeter is surrounded by a simple, five-foot brick wall, easy to jump over, guessing of course there's no underground electric wires or alarms. Other than those few things, the compound wasn't much different than what I would have expected to see or remember from the last time I was outside. I probably could have walked off the campus, but I felt no need to.

Instead, I sat in the grass staring at the sky, waiting for something to tell me what to do next. As I watched the clouds float by, I remembered that Jane once told me that if I looked at the sky for a long enough time, the chances were she'd be looking at it with me. I wonder if she ever did look at the sky today, for I was staring for quite a while. Something tells me that she did and that she knew I was looking too, but I could be wrong and just full of wishful thinking, either way nothing bad came of my actions and I rather enjoyed them as well.

By the time I came inside the sun had already set and I was hungry. I got to the cafeteria just in time for tuna sandwiches and soup. I love the tuna sandwiches, but the soup often times has the taste of motor oil, so I avoid it whenever possible.

I suppose that my day was filled with thinking 'n' such like it usually is, but with a mixture of mild activity, so it was good. Tomorrow I have an appointment with Dr. Shutz; I look forward to it and will write about it tomorrow…Bright day.

5/12 7:38 p.m.

Today was my appointment.

I saw Dr. Shutz today, and this is the gist of what happened:

"Hello, how are you today?" He asked me.

"I'm about as good as can be expected."

"And how exactly is that?"

"Well seeing since I'm in an institution, I have no freedom, I'd like to be elsewhere, and I don't really think there's anything wrong with me…I'm rather…discontent."

"Discontent, hmm…I thought you knew and accepted why you were here and agreed that it would be safer for everyone else as well."

"Oh I know why I'm here, I just don't want to be…"

"Then why are you here?"

"Because my mom wouldn't leave me alone."

"We've talked about this, you have to take responsibility for your actions, you cannot blame other people. Part of living in this world is putting up with the people that you'd rather not put up with."

"…I know…but it's still easier to blame others…"

He shot me a look and I knew that that's not what I should have said.

I continued. "Ok, so I suppose I could have had *more* control. But that's no longer the point, the point is, what do I do now and how do I fix myself?"

"Yes you could have had more control…I'm glad you're seeing part of the point. You're finally taking *some* responsibility."

"Oh I am, it's only taken me how long now?"

"Several years. No one ever said realization and recovery would be easy you know."

"Yeah, at least I'm noticing these things. When I first came here I wouldn't even talk to you about *any* of this let alone point out my own mistakes...now you are like my best friend."

"I'm glad you feel that way, but I'm hoping, in a good way, that my friendship to you is more short-term."

"I agree...but back to that point thing...what do I do next?"

"Well it seems that next you need to change your attitude towards people and violence in general, that way at least you'll think before you act and not generalize people so much. Also, having a positive attitude and perhaps some empathy would help a lot."

"Sounds like a plan, how do I start?"

"I can't direct your thinking, only you can do that...it's up to you...I can just give you ideas like I just did..."

The rest of my session was along the lines of that, and involved me explaining to him how my thoughts and things of this nature had been lately. I told him about my feelings about missing my friends, wanting my life back etc. I had no outbursts this time and I am glad to say the least. I suppose that maybe I am growing closer to my "escape" of this place.

As far as that goes, I suppose I'm going to have to see what happens, play-it-by-ear sort of thing. For I am moody, and I have no idea what is to come next. Until then, maybe I'll just go think...

5/13 10:11 p.m.

Michael Lee

Today I thought.

Silence

Sshh...
This is a quiet time,
There's nothing you need to do
And there's nothing you need to say

Silence yourself!
Clear your mind!
I said, don't think!
It's easier this way
This is how you meditate
This is how you become invincible
Now you can learn *yourself*
Just ask these questions -

How do I work?
How do others see me?
Am I a good person, or am I bad?
Do I need to change?
I don't know yet,
I'll just have to wait
To see the answer,
During my silence...

Sshh!
This is *my* quiet time!
There's something I need to do
But I don't know what to say

Why am I here? I mean, I know why I'm here, but why
have I decided to stay here for so long? I'm not really too
messed up, I only have fits when I'm under stress. But then

26

again, is there ever any stress in a setting such as this? I suppose not. Maybe if I exposed myself to stressful situations, such as interaction!? But will that be enough? The kind of stress I don't like involves stupid people, too much work, and interruptions of that work, and…well I guess pretty much any kind of hassles, I wonder if interaction will be enough to test that? Hmm, perhaps I'll give that a try sometime soon. As far as that goes, I'll have to play it by ear. But then what happens? What if I am exposed to stress again, how do I handle it? Apparently, screaming and violent reactions are not exactly those that are accepted readily in society. In fact, I don't think they ever were, so I guess I should let go of that and try to…vent…in other ways. But I do, that's what I do with this journal; I rationalize, justify, and think out my problems. My poetry is for that too, but then again that just ends up being angst poetry that confirms my already existent spite. Maybe if I attempted to write "Happy Poems," things would turn out better? Maybe if someone seemed to *care*, save for Dr. Shutz, I would do better. But no, people cared exponentially *before* I was in here and I still am, so I guess other people is not the answer? Hmm, could stability possibly come from within? Where within? My mind of course…what part of my mind? How do I find that stability? Why do people take that stability away from me? I let them. I don't want to let them; it's not nice to be without stability, for stability saves us all. So does good Karma. I need better Karma. Meditation is the key! Actually…maybe I should meditate on a more regular basis like this, instead like I normally do: "I hate people, people hate me, let's sit here and sulk." Now, let's find out how to stop hating people. I don't enjoy hate, although it is simple. But, simple is never the right way, you don't learn by doing simple tasks, you learn through being challenged. I have no motivation though. Wait, yes I do, to escape this place once and for all. Where should I go after that? I have no talents or redeeming qualities. I have nice hair? I don't like what color my hair is anyway, so nevermind, I have bad hair. Rrr, that's bad, to think that way I mean. Everyone has good qualities; God can't possibly be that cruel. I mean, in the largest general respect possible, men and women have good looks, a good brain, or large genitals – never all at once. On average everyone only has about one of those, porn stars for example have large genitals but are ugly and stupid. My friend Will over there is drop-dead-gorgeous but he is a catatonic, which cancels out the penis size because he'd never be able to use it. And then there's me for example, I give myself credit – for self-esteem reasons – and say I am of average looks, have a small penis, but am very intelligent according to my IQ Tests (148). Hmm, I guess there is something I can do with that right? Who the hell knows what though, I don't even know what I want. I had always planned to do something in computers because I am able to grasp the programming languages, operating systems, and multiple interfaces very easily. Either that or music because I love music…wonder if I can still play the French horn anymore. Oh well, not much I can do about any of that while I'm in here can I, guess I'll get out sooner than later.

Mmm, ink cartridge is running low and my room is too far away, plus I'm a bit hungry. The Doc mentioned something about a free-day coming up, maybe I'll write then? I don't know, anyway, I'm goin

The typewriter runs out of ink, so He quickly yanks the page out of the roller, puts it down next to Him, and stares off blankly. Then, as if bitten on the butt by an ant, jumps up and walks casually against the wall to the cafeteria to see what will be for lunch. Grilled ham and cheese sandwiches.

2
And then there was Light

Today was a long day.

I haven't written in a few days because nothing interesting has happened until today.

Well, first, two nights ago I finally decided to forgive and forget as much as I possibly can. I'm not sure why, but I'm sure it's because I'm sick of living like this and I want to move on with my life. Living in my introvert's sorry excuse for a world no longer appeals to me. I do not like sitting alone all of the time, subject to my own horrid thoughts. For one, my thoughts are monotonous, and as much as I hate change, I would like at least some kind of diversity to fall through my sieve of a brain. Secondly, I used to be a very social person; in fact, I was even considered fun to be around. But now, I am merely a fly on the wall that someone would rather smack, because of its depressing nature, than they would, want to talk to it. Therefore, I conclude that I do not like this solo existence.

I probably have a lot of steps to complete before I am over everything. Also, there's that wonderful "recovery" stage I have to deal with, but I think I can safely say that I am no longer hopeless. Dr. Shutz was very happy to hear me say that, and decided to give me a "field trip" day of my own – if I wanted it. I of course would have to bring one of the orderlies along with me just for safety reasons etc., but after thinking about it, I decided that I would take him up on his offer in the interest of becoming more social and to get out of my room.

So, last night I went to bed around ten p.m. instead of one or two A.M., and woke up at eight a.m., instead one or two p.m. I was very proud of myself and very excited about the upcoming day to say the least. I was actually surprised that my changed sleeping schedule didn't deprive me of energy, I guess that's what it feels like to sleep like a normal person? Anyway, they allowed me to wear some of my old civilian clothes; they barely fit, but I used to like them tight, so it was like I was a teen all over again. I got my backpack, filled it with snacks from the Cafeteria, my wallet (which had twenty dollars left in it from my last allowance), and a bottle of root beer.

Duncan and I got into the hospital van and began driving towards town. We first went to the old Monster Movie Theater that was once the popular high school scene and watched the movie, "In the Lions' Den." Over all, it was a good movie even though I did not recognize any of the actors. It was a mystery about some guy that was murdered by a large city gang and the private investigator that was trying to find out "who done it." There was a lot of gunfights and in the end the private investigator was killed, but not before convicting one of the murderers and pleasing the family of the victim.

We then went to the Frozen Cow, which is considerably more rundown than it was the last time I was there, but is still there nonetheless. Duncan, whose first name I found out is Al, ordered a large Peanut Butter Utter. I ordered a large Brownie Moo-Pie; complete with marshmallow sauce, brownie chunks, and whipped cream all over vanilla ice cream. Oh how delicious it was, I savored every spoonful of it, for we never get very much sugar at the hospital. Almost took me an hour just to finish it, I loved it, and I miss it already. Al and I sat outside talking and debating ideas of what to do next, which, after a movie and food, becomes even more difficult to do. Not thinking of anything to do, we sat and talked.

I found out that he was going through college to become a Psychology teacher, and that the job he had now was not permanent, that in fact, he might be gone within the year. He seemed very wise for his age and in some ways very much like me, only more stable. His apathetic attitude somehow only related to himself; he seemed interested in other people. I told him the short version of my life-story, and he told me a few unrelated stories of his own. There is much more to him than meets the eye, but it's more of a feeling I get than it is something I can explain. I like him a lot and hope that I'll see and talk to him more.

The sky was devoid of clouds today and I could see every single airplane flying above, no matter how high. The intricate ballet being performed by the crisscrossing contrails of the jet engines was interesting to watch and kept me entertained. But, with my short attention span I lost interest in the sky after about thirty minutes and moved on to bigger better things. It's funny, last time I checked, it was not recommended that you eat, change your radio station, do your make-up, *and* drive all at the same time. But, people do it anyway; it's a wonder they don't have more accidents than they already do. I guess the people in this world will never cease to amaze me. For the rest of the day, we rode around town visiting the various places that I used to spend most of my time. For most of the trip I sat staring out the window, reminiscing about the "good ol' days." I wished that Isaac and Frank were there to share the moment with me, but oh well, they were with me in my imagination, so that makes it ok.

I visited my old high school too. I loved that school, I spent my best moments in life there. I remember when Isaac and I used to spend everyday of school together and sometimes even after school just talking about only God knows what.

We'd talk about the meaning of life, our constant girl problems, how laughably simple or insanely difficult a class was, what we had for lunch, and even about the gum on the bottom of our shoes – There was this one time…nevermind. We had known each other for twelve years, and were best friends all twelve of those years. I wonder what happened to him…I miss that little ape-man. I'm kind of sad now, but that's OK, I'll see him again one of these days…that's what they invented the Internet for, right?

It turns out today is Wednesday, who knew, so Al took me to church and I actually met up with some of my old friends there! I was ecstatic when I saw them; it brightened my day even more. We all sat and talked for almost an hour outside during the service and caught up on each other's lives. They all said that they miss me and wish that I would get out soon to come see them more. I promised them that I would start trying to help myself to get out of this emotional hole, and that I would be out of here within a year. I really hope I can; I think this time I mean it too, I'm ready for a change, no matter how hard it may be; it's worth it.

Brittany gave me a lot of encouragement, most of which consisted of hugs and kisses, only some verbal. She used to live next door to me when we were little kids. I remember taking a bath with her when I was about five years old, before I knew it was supposed to be sexual – unfortunately. She grew up to be one of the most popular girls in school, damned sexy too. I once wanted to go out with her in eighth grade, but we decided not to because it would ruin our friendship. For the next two years, nothing changed between us except that we got a bit closer as friends. It's strange, I never really did learn *too* much about her, mostly just surface things. So far as trust and all that is concerned though, she was like the sister I never got to have. I miss her a lot, more than the others, for like I have said before, church people are fake and I don't put too much effort into deep relationships with them; she is different.

32

After that, it was almost time for curfew so Al took us home...here. Home, God I hope not. We got back with no problems and after they collected my personal items, I went back to my room to think; thus coming up with my above resolve to get better faster and sooner.

Other than that though, today was a lot of walking and observing. I'm going to go to BED now...Yep, that's right, I'm going to attempt to use the bed today...I don't know how it'll turn out...but it might be fun...I'll write about it tomorrow as long as I don't die...until then...Good night.

5/19 11:57 p.m.

Today was fun.

In my recent decision to start getting better, I've also decided to be more extroverted, to sort of relearn how to interact with society. So today, instead of sitting in my corner watching the people go by, I decided that I would join them in *their* daily routines instead indulging in my monotonous one.

When I got up and walked across the room to go to the chess table, the people that have been here long enough to know what I'm like, stopped what they were doing, and watched me cross the room. I don't think I've ever felt more self-conscious in my life, but I kept walking because today I was determined to interact. I sat down in the chair across from the man that was playing chess with himself – Sisal. I have seen him before, and as far as I can tell, he is here because he is manic-depressive. Not just your everyday manic-depressive, his manic moods usually involve extreme violence, then when he's calm he concentrates obsessively and calmly on things like string and ceiling bumps – very intelligent person. Because of this, there must be an orderly assigned to him at all times – Lithium rarely works. Anyway, I asked him if I could play a game and he said sure, so we set up the pieces and got to it.

I won the first game by using a three-move checkmate that Isaac taught me a long time ago. When he looked up, he smiled, but a more evil smile than I thought was necessary; I quickly asked for another game. He liked the idea, and in the interest of keeping my limbs intact, I let him win a few times, but also beat him like a, "red headed step child," enough times to keep my self-esteem intact. At first, we were both very quiet, but I soon was entranced in one of the longer games and started growling and cackling whenever a good move was made by either of us. I eventually began feeling very open, and started making loud snide remarks – not at him, at the pieces, because they are the ones that are doing the actual killing. I mostly pleaded with them not to hurt my army, but they did not relinquish their hold on my men. So as a diversion I pretended to be hurt and when they least expected it, destroyed them! I used some Russian war tactics that I learned about in World History, and in the end they proved of no help. I forgot that Russians, much like Canadians and the French, have never really done anything on their own except own gigantic, empty countries – just kidding.

I finally looked up, only to notice that a few people were watching us. Normally I would have stopped and hidden, but I was feeling extraordinarily courageous today, so I continued with my strange noises, remarks, and tactics. The next game was actually much more heated than the rest because we were both developing complex strategies, planning ahead, and tricking each other with each move; it was great! I was intent on winning this battle though, for our day had been long; score fourteen to fourteen. However, this time it was no longer about the pieces and chess, it was more so a battle of wits and intelligence between Sisal and me, and I refuse to ever lose a battle of such things.

In fact, my entire life I have never minded losing anything *except* a battle of wits and intelligence. For this is the one thing that I have left in my life – especially now – and I hold my remaining confidence to my ability to be more intelligent than the majority of the people in a room or other related community place. According to the I.Q. Test I took upon entrance of this place, I am eight points above the beginning of the "gifted" scale.

Anyway, we were both down to two pieces, which ironically were the King and Queen for both of us. We played cat and mouse for almost ten minutes until I broke his concentration and killed his queen. I look back now and see that screaming, "LOOK IT'S JESUS!" was not so much a good idea, but I'm not dead, so I suppose it's ok. When I looked up, all of the people in the room were standing around us watching or looking for Jesus – depending on their disorder. The attention felt familiar, but I was more nervous about them than I was about the game at that point. I tried to ignore the people and continue the game; his King evaded my Queen for what seemed like forever, but finally I cornered him, and when I did, I yelled "CHECK MATE!" as loud as I possibly could, then skipped around the room singing a victory song. Any other time everyone would have thought that I was crazy, but since I am already in the "funny farm," no one really thought it strange. Several of the less coherent people joined in my dancing and yelling until some of the nurses came over to see what was the matter. I told them of my triumph and they seemed decidedly unmoved. I didn't care though; I was intent on thoroughly enjoying my winnings. I probably should be more careful around Sisal though, I remember a rather frightening scowl appearing on his face during my charade, but yet again no violence – maybe he likes me.

Dr. Shutz was very happy when he heard the news, but warned me that it could possibly be the effect of the pills. Anyway, my day was good; I liked it whether the pills were involved or not…Wonderful day!

5/21

Today was my birthday?

It seems that today was my birthday. The only reason I know this is because Dr. Shutz showed me my file. Him and a few other patients and nurses threw me a small birthday party that consisted of a cake and two presents; I had fun.

On my daily journey to the game room after getting dressed etc., I was surprised by Al, Benny, Robert, Malcolm, Dr. Shutz, and several other nurses, who were all wearing party hats and were standing around a table that had a cake and oddly wrapped presents on it. They sat me down in front of the cake, turned out the lights, and sang happy birthday. Unfortunately though, I was not allowed to have lit candles because it is a fire hazard, but I pretended they were lit, just for fun. Nurse Joy distributed the cake out to everyone that wanted and or could have some, and we all ate.

My first present was from Dr. Shutz; it was an electric Notebook with a magnetic pen. A very sensible gift, I now know why he kept asking me how I was liking the journal idea and why he asked to read some of my entries. I told him that I was enjoying it, but that the typewriter that I use jams quite often because it's old, and I can not always finish or even write some entries – very frustrating. Also, if I make a mistake, I am unable to delete it. It also seems that he gave me one of the better electric Notebooks because this one has the option that allows me to change my hand-written words to type. Also, the electric one is much better because with paper and pencil my hand will smear everything across the page – being left-handed is great but has its set-backs as well. Plus, along with one hundred of the electric pages, there are one hundred paper pages you can rip, out there is a pocket for other things as well. This notebook will prove to be a great tool.

My second gift was a hand-drawn picture of a beautiful landscape, I never knew Robert was such an artist.

I enjoyed my birthday and hope that I have more. Oh yeah, almost forgot, I turned twenty-one years old! Now I'm old enough to drink and drive! Heh, I'm going to go, nothing else to talk about except that Sisal and I now plan to play Chess everyday when we're both mentally stable, and I'm happy about that, I guess you can call him a new friend. Good day!

5/23/10 4:25 p.m.

I feel devious today.

I haven't written in a few weeks because the whole purpose of this journal is to describe my day in a calm way so that I don't overreact and go crazy etc., etc. And, since nothing really bad or disappointing has happened lately, I haven't felt the need to write.

My games with Sisal are going well, and have actual turned into tournaments; thus, I've made a couple of new friends. I'm really nervous when I'm around them, and I'm not sure how to act or what to say. It's not exactly easy to be friends with mentally unstable people to begin with, especially if you're one of them, but I'll manage. I've been sleeping less and less lately, and doing more and more. I've started going outside a lot, but often times come back in quickly because of the unbearable heat, humidity, and lack of clouds – I like to watch clouds. The only good thing about the weather outside is, if the air conditioning is on too strong or if I feel the need to stare at the daytime moon. Oh well, there's plenty to do inside like...play chess...and...watch people play chess...ok yeah it's not as great here as I thought it was.

On a more serious side, I haven't taken my pills since the day after I started interacting with people. I've been doing the "under the tongue and spit out later" trick. I haven't noticed much change though, except that I've been a bit more enthusiastic about things, a lot less tired, and a few other minor things that seem to be positive effects instead of negative ones. It's still too early to tell if I can handle it, but I'm confident that I can and will. I guess I'll eventually have to tell Dr. Shutz, hopefully he'll take it well, and maybe I can get out of here soon? Who knows, I guess I'll just have to wait, but until then, I'll have to hide this entry just to make sure he doesn't find out prematurely…I'll write later…Be afraid?

6/8

I have a routine.

My daily routine is rather monotonous and predictable, but because I'm bored, I'll write about it anyway.

I begin my day anytime between seven a.m. and two p.m., which is good, accordingly to one of the few magazines I'm exposed to, waking up between those times makes for the most energized and awake days. I'm not sure why, but I think it has something to do with sun light and oxygen intake to the brain. In fact, I've noticed an increase in my mood even from waking up at that time.

Anyway, I then go to the bathroom to do my morning cleaning ritual; straighten out my arm hair, wash the crap out of my eyes, shave if I need to, and pee.

Then, I go to the Cafeteria for breakfast or lunch, depending on which I wake up for, I get the same thing weekly, not because I want to and am compulsive, but because I have no real choice, except on the type of milk – Whole or 2%, I prefer 2%. At that same time I take my pills and sit down to eat. The lunch ladies do not seem to care that I hate mixing my food, so I spend the next five minutes or so separating everything out so that none of it is touching. If anything is mixed permanently, I won't eat it because it's gross.

After eating, I walk through the hallway in search of something to do. More often than not, I end up in the game room, where, before Sisal, I would sit and watch people from the corner on the same side of the wall as the TV. There, I would attempt to figure everyone out, stare off blankly, or think about the recent week or events in my life. Now though, I sit at the Chess table waiting for a challenger or for Sisal.

After a certain said number of games I walk back 'n forth in the halls looking for something to do, but usually end up in my room, writing about my day or what I've been thinking about recently. Then I eat dinner and again sit in the game room or my room, thinking, or writing. I've recently been going outside more though, and I'll do that usually before dinner, however, I haven't been outside at night in a while, so I think that tonight I will – in fact, right now.

He closes His notebook and, taking it with Him, walks through the ward to the front desk. The nurse there gives Him permission to go outside for thirty minutes, so He signs out, walks to the front gate, gives the orderly there His "Outdoor Pass," and proceeds to find an open place in the grass to lay down.

Wow! It *has* been a long time since I've been outside this late. It's amazing, from here you can see almost all of the stars. It's a much different night out here than it is inside the city, you can hear the sounds of animals, the rustling trees, and can even see some of the orbiting satellites. It is indeed amazing what God has made, despite my discontentment for his people and his rules.

Hmm…

He continues to gaze upon His surroundings until an orderly finds Him then sends Him inside again.

I feel drained today.

I haven't written in several days for a very good reason that I'll explain in a minute, but first I just want to say that I won't give up.

I've been in solitary confinement for the last few days because I went out of control when someone started making fun of me.

I played Ping-Pong today even though I'm not very good at it and like to play around and act stupid instead. Often times I hit the ball as hard as I can and then act proud of myself for making it fly across the room. Or, what I sometimes like to do is put two tables together and play across them. Now, my partner was all for that idea, but some people didn't seem to think it was as funny as we did. So someone, I think it was Richard, started making-fun of me for being an idiot. Normally people making fun of me is no big deal because it happens often and no longer bothers me. But then he started insulting my intelligence and telling me that I am a hermit and will never get out of here because I don't have the guts to go back to the real world. I put up with his heckling for what seemed like forever, but I couldn't handle it anymore and he was getting other people to laugh at me too, so I exploded on him.

Not only did I cuss him out, but I also jumped on him and tried to choke him to death, anything to get him to shut up. I was nearly successful in killing the asshole, but right about the time he was pleading for me to stop I was ripped off of him by four orderlies and put into a straight jacket. Another thing I absolutely hate is not being in control of my own body, so naturally I screamed and kicked just like in the movies.

They decided to put me into solitary confinement for two days because I was screaming inane babble about how everyone hates me despite my efforts to fit-in. Of course, at the time I'm sure I wasn't near as calm and wasn't probably making much sense either, so it was probably better for me to stay there. Plus it doesn't help that, after the normal two hours, I was still agitated and semi-out-of-control, to say the least, so they decided to keep me in. Little do they know, if they had sent me to my own room and taken me out of the jacket I'd have been fine, but oh well, that's their job I guess.

Fortunately though, Dr. Shutz finally came to see me and I felt better as soon as I saw him. I decided that now was a good time to inform him that I hadn't been taking my pills anymore. He was disappointed to say the least, and after a long conversation, said that we'll never know if the medicine was successful in suppressing extreme feelings of anger or not. The pills were to act as a control in the experiment and Richard was the variable. Experiments do not work with two variables. I told him I was sorry and that I'd go back on the meds as soon as possible, but that'd I'd like to continue to try to help myself to get out of here with limited drug interference. He said that he was glad that I decided to continue, but thought it would be in my best interest to take a few days to think about my outburst before I return to the group. He said it was up to me when I was ready to come out, and agreed that I should wait a while to get back to my "friends." As far as the pills were concerned, we decided to lower the dosage considerably and see what happens, but that I should keep doing what I was doing so that we could continue the "experiment."

So here I am now, on my floor, tired as hell from a dull ten-hour day of sitting, thinking, writing, and pacing. I think I'll go to bed soon, and depending on how I feel tomorrow, depends on what I'll do...maybe I'll go outside and walk around? Err, I have a migraine, perhaps I'll stay inside and sleep instead...oh well whatever, good night, long day.

6/12 midnight

Today was exciting.

Personally, I think today was the best day I've had in a long time. I woke up around six A.M., which is a good start, and decided to take a jog. I'm not sure why, but I remember

41

that during the summer I used to run almost every morning before it got too hot. It would make me feel nice and would give me energy to do things for the rest of that day, not to mention get me into shape and loosen tense muscles.

When I went out to run, I noticed it was raining, I *love* summer rain, the warm drops falling through the cool morning air is so soothing and peaceful to me. There weren't many people outside in the rain, so it was quiet, which makes it all so much better. The pitter-patter of the drops against the building and the ground were like music to my ears – I could have melted right there. It was nice to say the least, and I would have run longer if it weren't for the fact that I'm not so much in shape as I used to be. So I probably only ran about a quarter of a mile or so around the building before I grew tired and out of breathe.

After running, I walked around and semi-danced in the rain while humming to myself, then came inside, went to the cafeteria, and took my morning pills. Turns out today is June fourteenth (not sure why that's important), so the meals for the day were all special. For breakfast I ate nicely made pancakes, scrambled eggs, toast, and milk! That there is my favorite breakfast of all time! I took my time savoring each delicious syrup covered square of pancake, every voluptuous chunk of scrambled egg, and each delectable bite of jam covered toast, then washed it all down with a tall glass of wonderful 2% milk. Mmm, I'm getting hungry all over again...

Anyway, after breakfast, I sat down in front of the TV – evil I know, but I needed to rest and no one was up to play games with – and found a 24-Hour Scooby-Doo Marathon! I was so excited that I screamed! I've loved that show ever since I was a kid, I can't believe it's still on, I guess TV isn't so horrible after all. I immediately jumped and sat directly underneath the TV, crossed my legs, and watched intently for what seemed like the whole day. In reality though, it had only been about three hours, but it was lunchtime and I was hungry anyway, so I decided to take a break from the TV so that my retinas wouldn't burn; I headed for the cafeteria again.

That's when the best part of the day happened! As I was walking towards the Cafeteria, a group of people at the front desk caught my eye. I started to look away because there's normally a lot of people there anyway, but one of them looked very familiar to me, so I gave them all a second glance. I couldn't believe it, it was Jane, Isaac, Frank, and Lea! I hadn't seen them all in almost two years! I was so happy and excited that I ran up to them as fast as I could and gave them all hugs before they even knew it was me!

We all ate lunch, bacon cheeseburgers with veggies, and they explained that they had been told by a little birdie that I was doing a lot better and was stable enough to be visited again. I was glad to hear that they were all still living in town and that they all talked to the same birdies that I do. They looked at me wonderingly and I smiled to signify that I was not crazy and knew that there were no *actual* birds that could talk – except Bill. ☺

We all watched Scooby-Doo together for an hour or so, played games, played outside, and then sat in my room talking. Apparently, Isaac is a bossonova Ping-Pong player so he whooped on all of us. It was quite fun though because the majority of the time I had him chasing after the ball and or my paddle. Frank watched TV mostly because, for as long as I can remember, he's been addicted to it. He changed the channel from Scooby-Doo and I about went nuts, but strangely, Lea was more into it than I was and she made him change it back. It's amazing the kind of things you can get being a girl, I wish I was one! Ok no. Jane was just having a lot of fun watching us because she's always wanted to be a psychologist, which is why she helped me as much as she did. Hell, without her I'd probably be in a straight jacket a LOT more often than I am now.

In fact, if I had never met her I'd probably be in jail for killing my entire family right now. She's the one that never gave up on me and taught me that love comes in many shapes and sizes. The outcome – hurting my mom etc. – happened despite her teachings, but I at least know how to think a bit more clearly now – as far as my inner monologue is concerned.

Anyway though, not one-second of the day went by that someone wasn't talking, which is good because I miss and love talking. It was like old times again, it made me feel very special and important and wonderful the whole time they were here. They apologized for not visiting anymore and I apologized for getting myself into trouble to begin with and for being an ass the last time they all were here – long story – and all was good. It's nice to forgive, forget, and move on. Most of the day with them would take forever to explain in detail, but I'll just say that my hope has been renewed again and that I'm going to try to be "cured" even harder than I've already resolved to be.

The guys told me that they have an extra room in their apartment for me, and Jane said she always has room for me in her heart, mind, and phone line. I don't really know Lea very well because she's Frank's girlfriend, but she said from all the stuff he's told her, that she thinks I'll make a "startling recovery." I was encouraged by their words to say the least, and I think I will hopefully soon take them up on their offers.

It was late by the time they left, so in the interest of finishing my day on a good note I finished watching the Scooby-Doo Marathon, and wrote one of my best "Happy Poems," that I've written in a long long time.

Friends

Friends are the people that;
Greet you with a hug
Or a special hand-shake

They are the ones that say bye
With a funny wave
Or an ever bigger hug than before

Friends are the people that;
Laugh with you when having fun
And laugh at you when making fun
But of course you don't mind
Because, you're friends

Friends are the people that;
Share life's stories
Or food when you're hungry
And money if you're lucky
As long as you pay them back

Friends are the people that;
Are there when you cry
And join in without knowing why
Then help you through it
And wipe the tears and fears – Away

And best of all –
Friends are the ones that;
Through all of life's troubles
And little or big obstacles
Never forget you
And you never forget,
Because they will always be your – Best Friends

...Mmm, I've written better, but I like it...heh it's almost one A.M., and I'm still smiling, but I'm tired as hell, so I think I'll go to sleep. But tonight's sleep will be different...because I'm going to sleep in the bed, and I'm going to *enjoy* it...Wait until I tell Dr. Shutz about my day! Goodnight.

6/15 12:48 a.m.

I'm bored.

The air conditioning broke today and again I am hot, sweaty, and annoyed.

I'm sitting here in my underwear with the barred window open, fanning myself with a stack of typing paper in one hand, and am writing with the other. I really have no reason to write today except that no one else is outside of their rooms, because only their rooms have windows, and it is too hot to move, play games, or sit anywhere without being clothed, and that is strictly against the rules. Oh great, I have to pee now and I really don't feel like getting up at the moment, oh well, I'll do it later.

Anyway, it's been a couple of days since my friends came to see me and I miss them a lot right now. I've been thinking a lot about all of the things we used to do, especially the summer before my junior year of high school. It was the summer I got my first job, the summer I lost my virginity to the one girl I loved, and the summer that all hell broke lose. My old friend Jonathan (he's a Marine now) and I, decided that we were bored, much like today, and rented a wood chipper. It was expensive, but together we were able to pay for one hour of use without going broke.

It was the most fun we'd ever had. After hooking it up to his POS pick-up, we dragged the thing all the way over to my house and began throwing as much as possible into it. We started by shredding all of the empty cardboard boxes that were taking up space in the garage, and actually cleaned up enough of those to put half of the unused junk in my room, into the newly made empty spaces. Next, we graduated to all of the stupid self-help and anger management books my parents had gotten me. I read most of them and found them of no use, so we shredded them. I found my broken Nintendo behind the TV, and sent that through it, it's amazing how strong those wood chippers are. It turned the Nintendo into plastic dust and chunks of silicon. By that time, I was beginning to run out of expendable objects so we decided to clean out the fridge. My parents used to buy me tons of food that I would never eat, so we threw a watermelon through it – awesome explosion. I can't remember most of the rest, but I know there were stuffed animals, old toys, and other related breakable, shreddable items. After about an hour of all this though, we realized that we had run out of ideas when we sent a bunch of pencils through it; nothing happened. We returned the chipper and the guy was a little bit disturbed at how dirty it was and asked us what we had put through it. We told him our whole list and he seemed oddly ok with all of it until we told him about the watermelon and bottle of ketchup. Supposedly, you're not supposed to put liquidy items through it, especially one's that are sticky and hard to clean up. We gave him twenty dollars to make up for it and he sent us on our way. It's a good thing we didn't put the neighbors dog and or any siblings through it as we had originally planned or there would have been a bigger mess, not to mention the fact that it's illegal, but oh well who cares.

Heh, I wish I could rent a wood chipper now, I'd have thrown my mattress and nightstand through it just to watch them get eaten alive. Oh well, I REALLY need to pee now, so I'm going to go, hot day!

6/19

Today was horrible.

I haven't written in almost three weeks because I've been so busy and happy with Sisal that I haven't had the time or a reason to write – until today.

Today I received news, by word of mouth, that my dad died two days ago – he was sixty-three. The only word I can think of to describe the way I feel right now is…devastated.

This news does not help my state of mind at all, for I am still very fragile and am not yet immune to stress, nor close to being so. I've never really lost someone close to me like this before and I used to be strong about such things – but am no longer. I'd have been able to handle this a few years ago without reacting the way that I did/am right now. When I heard about my dad's death, I fell to the floor because I no longer had the strength or the will to stand and I began crying and screaming hysterically. The orderlies had to drag me back to my room – I put up no fight.

It's ironic the way things work. I do not like family because I have seen it tear so many peoples' lives apart and have had it tear mine apart as well. Family are the people that you are born with, live with, and die with, but *that* should be as far as it goes. All too often, family is the one that drives its members to suicide and or destroys itself and those that are in the wake. Family to me, is the gum on the bottom of my boot, they are an annoyance that slows me down, and when melting, completely cover and wreck that boot. For they criticize what you do in the name of love, stop you from doing what you want in the name of concern, and worst of all, love you only because they "have to," not because they want to.

No, I'm sorry but I put a LOT more stock into that of friendship, for they are the people who will not leave me to myself, will love me because they want to, and will help me through things with unconditional positive regard. They are the ones that support me and have supported me through everything in my life. However difficult it was for them, and for me, they are the ones who have not left me in spirit or in mind.

I see myself being contradictory, but that is because my dad is not family, he is my dad. There is a fine line between the two. For the fact that my dad was not always a moral man and cheated on my mother – I don't blame him because she is a bitch that needs to die...umm, that needs to be of leaving me alone...- they separated when I was very young. Strangely, I never found that unusual, maybe because the divorce rate was seventy-eight percent, or maybe because I was sick of hearing the screaming, either way it never bothered me...that I am aware of. But because of this, my dad and I forged a relationship that was more of a best friend relationship than it was that of the domineering father. Because of that, he has never been part of my family, but instead, that of the coolest person and or friend that I have...had. I miss him...

Anyway though, I've gone through the stages of accepting this particular death like clockwork: First fear, denial, then anger, and now helplessness and sorrow.

Stages of Death

Fear
Denial
Anger
Acceptance
The stages of death.
Do you know them?
Do you want to know them?
Who will show you?
I won't show you,
I'm alive!
Don't be offended
I'm not joking,
I'm not mocking,
I'm not contagious
You don't know?
I'm sick!
I'm dying!

I'm sick of dying!
It hurts!
Make it stop!
Please help me!?
You can't...
I understand,
Give me my friends
I have something to say

Thank you,
I love you
I'll miss you
Good luck to your lives,
Good bye,
I know the stages of death
Because I've died...

Anyway, It will probably be a very long time before I decide to accept what has happened, so for now, I will sulk in my own self-pity and hope that no one decides to talk to me, for I am uncertain what will happen when they do.

In the interest of keeping others and myself safe, I've remade my "bubble," only this time the bubble that I stay in is real. While in the cafeteria I grabbed enough packets of sugar to create a large semi-circle around the corner of my room. This semi-circle is my bubble; nothing can touch me – not the real world, not anything, nor anyone. I feel safe and comfortable being naive and ignorant of my immediate surroundings, and I believe that in a strange sort of way, it protects me from the world and its evils.

Here I will stay, with my pillow, my notebook, and a pile of pencils, until *I* think that I am ready to come out. I've sent a note to Dr. Shutz through Duncan, asking if he can come here to hold my sessions, and that he also brings food with him when he comes. I will be eating and sleeping in my bubble for as long as Dr. Shutz or I think is necessary...although, I haven't figured out my arrangements for defecation yet...I'll work that out later.

The last time I did this, the bubble was in my mind because I had school to attend. I sent a message to each of my friends' desk computers, telling them that I didn't want to talk that day so that they wouldn't provoke me. I sat quietly in each class with a stone cut expression of dissatisfaction and anger. My friends luckily respected my wishes and in fact spoke for me when someone else that was not aware of my situation talked to me. At the moment, I can't remember what the reason for my discontent was, but I'm sure that it was something related to a girl because there was always something related to a girl back in-the-day.

...I miss my daddy, I hadn't seen him for several years, and the last time I saw him, I was grouchy and being mean...I'm sorry dad...

I can't write about this anymore, I'll try again later, it's not safe for me right now anyway...I must go, bad day.

7/2/10 2:38 a.m.

The next afternoon the door to His room opens and Doctor Shutz walks in with a trying smile and a hello. He moves across the room and stands several feet away from the ring of sugar, waiting for a response.

"Are you hungry?" asks Doctor Shutz.

"No..." He answers without looking away from His notebook.

An orderly walks in holding a plate and paper cup. He glances at the doctor and sets the food down outside of the sugar ring then leaves, closing the door behind him.

"I brought you food," says the doctor, hoping to attract attention.

"I'm not hungry..."

"It's your favorite, tuna sandwich, chips, and fruit punch. You need to eat something or you'll get sick."

He looks up only enough to see the plate; "Today is grilled cheese day..."

"I know, I had them make it special for you," says Doctor Shutz, hopefully.

He glances in the direction of the doctor then down at the plate. He sets the notebook down next to His pillow and leans over towards the edge of the ring. "Joom!" He grabs the plate and paper cup quickly, "JOOM!" then leans back, falling against the wall comfortably. He takes a bite of the sandwich, continuing to stare only at His food and at the floor directly in front of Him. He does not like the doctor seeing Him like this; it does not show good progress and could possibly disappoint the doctor, His best friend.

The doctor stares at his secretly favored patient quizzically, then asks Him if there is anything He'd like to talk about.

"No."

"Very well, you know how to find me if you do."

"Yeah..." He trails off and quickly looks to the doctor like a child looks at their parents when searching for approval.

The doctor smiles and heads for the door slowly. As He opens it, He hears a small voice, that of a twelve year old, saying thank you in a tone that suggests appreciation for more than just a sandwich and drink.

Doctor Shutz smiles triumphantly to himself, but says and does nothing, except for a pause in his steps. He thinks for a second and decides that there is still hope for this one, then walks out, closing the door behind him.

My dad.

I've come closer to accepting what's happened – I think. About as able as I ever will be to understanding and accepting the death of yet another person that I care about. Well, technically he is the first of my best friends to die; the others have only just died metaphorically because I do not see them very often. They have visited recently, as I wrote before, but that was almost a month ago now. Ok, so that's not very long ago, but right now it feels like it was forever ago, so I have the right to complain, don't I? No, I suppose not, they have lives too...or, *they* have lives. But that has nothing to do with the price of gas, this entry is supposed to be about my dad.

Towards the end, I hadn't talked to him much. After my sophomore year, he stopped coming out to see me because he was becoming increasingly poorer. His business had taken a turn for the worse, I guess they don't need Meals on Wheels in small town Iowa. His loan to the bank was barely paid off and he was late on several child-support payments. Usually he's not, he's a very responsible man – prison will do that to you – so that's how we knew something was wrong. Anyway, after paying off those debts he was broke, so he moved in with an old friend of his so that he could get back on his feet. All of that and more – which I never really did get straight – prevented him from coming to see me that summer.

So, in the interest of keeping myself busy, I got a job at the nearby grocery store as a stock boy. Good stuff, got me nice and strong, built, toned, and was a generally easy job, no stress. He called infrequently that summer and those calls became even more rare as the year continued. The summer ended and it was the first one I had ever had without seeing my dad. I was saddened to say the least. My junior year started with a kick because I asked out my co-stock girl, and she said yes.

We started "going out" with each other and the boyfriend girlfriend titles were bestowed upon us. I enjoyed the six months of attention, affection, love, communication, and fun times that we both provided for each other. Things were going great and as usual and I was becoming very attached to her, in a way that bordered, or might have been, obsession. She had had boyfriend problems in the past because guys are about the biggest MORONS in the world and trusted me to by a good guy – I eventually failed.

I mean, according to some survey I did once, over sixty percent of all guys are jerks! And, accordingly to *another* survey I did, this is because they disrespect girls and think with their dicks. I can't stand disrespect of any kind unless that particular person deserves it by being disrespectful in one way or another first. Heh, I used to say that all women would eventually train to be Amazon like women and destroy all men except Isaac, Frank, and I because we were the last of the good fellas. Then, us three would be responsible for repopulating the Earth, and in effect would all become obsessed with sex and would be killed by the Amazons ourselves, leaving the world in hopefully good hands (we would teach our offspring MORALS!). But of course, that wouldn't work because one of our kids would try to take over the world using explosions...JUST LIKE ON TV!

Oh my god! I just laughed, oh, but that is pretty funny.

...Rrr, where was I. Oh yeah, anyway, so she had trust problems, so, being the nice person that I am, I attempted to make her feel better, practically every night and strangely – I didn't think it was strange at the time – that feeling of being needed is what made me fall in love with her. I later discovered that she was a nervous, indecisive, dependent, little girl that could not figure out her own problems, was obsessed with making EVERYONE ELSE happy, and was self-destructive in all ways possible, to mention a few things. So, I'm rather glad that I didn't stay with her...not that I could, being in here anyway. But my point was...that she caused a lot of mental anguish that really wasn't worth it, and that, mixed with my hard classes, missing dad, before and after school activities, lack of sleep, and most of all, my mom, messed everything up!

Eh, Dr. Shutz just walked in...I really don't want him to see me like this, I'm sort of in a vulnerable state of mind. No I don't want to talk to you...I'm not hungry go away... Please, I don't want to do something I'll regret...I do like tuna... I can't

look at you I'm sorry, but you'll be disappointed...right?...
Thank you...

He left...and...heh...anyway, hmm, I strangely feel
better just from him coming in here, he cared enough to have
them make me a tuna sandwich when today is grilled cheese
day. See! That's the kind of stuff that I wish I had ALL the
time! Actually, I did have that all the time, whenever I was
with my dad...I guess Dr. Shutz is my adopted dad...or am I
his adopted son?

Mmm, he broke my concentration, jerk! Heh, just
kidding, he's cool.

Anyway, apparently my dad's money problems
subsided because he came here to see me about nine months
after I was admitted. Sadly though, I was still more than
spiteful about my situation and I blamed everyone for
everything. Only recently have I really discovered/admitted
that *I* am in control of *me*, not anyone else. However much I'd
like to say that it's everyone else's fault, it's not. But at the time
I didn't know this, so I was rude, intolerable, insufferable, and
just plain mean to him. He was here for only a short while and
the entire time he tried to cheer me up. It worked, but only for
a bit, mostly because I was fighting it, I didn't want to be happy
anymore, I just wanted to sit on my ass and be a jerk, it worked
– unfortunately.

He left and my mood had rubbed off onto him by
diffusion it seemed. I didn't care at the time, but a few days
later I ended up crying about it because I feared that he would
never return. I was right; however, I received many letters,
only some of which I responded to. I was not mad at him
though, so in every letter I tried to seem as cheery as possible
(if that was possible), and made them all the length of a book –
several needed two stamps. Strangely though, the letters came
less and less, and the last thing I knew, he was getting married
again. He seemed to have found a real winner, whatever the
hell that means – I don't put much faith into relationships

anymore, but I'm sure that would change if I found a girl I liked.

His last letter was more so a note than anything else, only a page long, telling me that everything was going ok and that he was happily married. It continued to explain that he was moving to California – what a dirty place to live – to start a new business, cleaning grocery carts, a real moneymaker. After that, I never received a change of address letter or anything else for that matter. I sent a couple letters to his old address hoping that maybe it would be forwarded, but those were all sent back.

I gave up on my dad and placed him in the back of my head as a, "Temporarily Out of Service Friend," a made up part of my brain where I keep my few good memories. After that I heard nothing until a few days ago, a letter from his widow, simply stating that of his death and how it happened – a drunk driver, the few that remain since the mass production and use of synthaholic drinks – a most dishonorable death for a man of his caliber. Hmph, it's amazing that someone still drinks that stuff. Since the legalization of many of the other less harmful drugs (speed, marijuana, ecstasy, and other such boring drugs), someone still chooses to use something that completely distorts all of your perceptions, reactions, and gives you a hang over the next day? Then, to make matters worse, drives around, only to smash into another car and kill the person inside – the drunk surviving of course. It truly bothers the piss out of me. Luckily though, I've been writing long enough today that I'm rather calm about it. I'd probably be rampaging through the room banging on things and yelling loudly about how evil the world is and why it is sending itself down a flaming spiral to Hell if I didn't have this journal to write in.

I guess that means this form of therapy is working.

Well, I'm feeling all writed out today, so I will retire to my corner again – sleepless night

7/3

3
Bouncing Back

Today is the 4th of July.

I woke up a few minutes ago to the loud sounds of firecrackers popping and crackling somewhere outside. I don't know what time it is because I've been falling asleep when I become bored or overwhelmed with thought. I imagine it's late though because there is no light coming from my window, and like I said, there are firecrackers being played with outside.

Sadly, the only firecrackers you can buy now-a-days are Poppers, everything else has been banned because within the last ten years more fires than the firemen would like to put out, have started and destroyed billions of dollars worth of property. Of course, there are still some counties throughout Tennessee and other redneck states that have legalized every single type of firecracker, including the M-1000, a ¾ stick of dynamite (good for destroying an entire plumbing network).

I've always liked Independence Day, it's when all of the good summer movies came out, it's when America came together for a day, it's when the weather was always just right, and it's what marked the beginning of a good summer. I've seen some pretty awesome fireworks before (professional companies are still allowed to use big ones), once in Louisville, once in Denver, and a few good ones here in town. Fireworks technology has always been something interesting to me, probably because I enjoy fire – it's pretty and sparkly – not because I'm a pyromaniac. I especially like the ones that create the little pictures in the sky because it's amazing how much time, effort, and money is put into making those ones. I once saw one that created a picture of George Washington standing on his boat on his way down the Delaware. I also remember this one really awesome

He slowly nods off to sleep, drops His pencil, and falls over onto His pillow once more.

Loneliness.

I find myself unable to sleep because, for the last few days, I have slept erratically. It's times like this that remind me I'm an only child, which, is actually better than having siblings, in my opinion. Many people disagree with me because they think only children turn out to be hermits and have other such social problems. My personal experience is to the contrary, for, while I was growing up as an only child I discovered many ways to keep myself busier than any brothers or sisters could ever find. Of course, the majority of the time I was building something, destroying something, or building something to destroy it. I suppose I just like breaking things, I mean, I find it funny when something gets destroyed (as long as no one is hurt). Like the time that I put my fist through the wall, because I was mad. After I realized there was a hole I was no longer mad but in fact was acting goofy and laughing hysterically while rolling around on the floor. At that particular time, Isaac and Jon were there, and they too found it hilarious. Of course, Jon had to ruin the fun by reminding me of my pending death by motherly strangulation. Oh well though, no matter, it was still fun. Or the time I destroyed a twenty-four pack of Diet Cola with a hammer...those were the days. But now, I sit in my room with no hammer, with unbreakably soft walls, and no one to egg me on. So, I sit here alone, as an only child amongst many brothers whom I am afraid to see or talk to. All I can do is think about nothing, listen to the crickets and bullfrogs outside, sulk, and wait. I have nothing really to write, so I believe I will attempt to get over this myself, without writing. If more entries on the subject of the death of my father appear later, it is because I was held hostage by my mind, and my hand will be scrolling lightly on electric paper purely by accident and against my will. Strange night.

7/5 4:58 a.m.

In remembrance of all whom I have lost.

I've been thinking a lot about school lately, remembering all of the good and bad times, of all the people I used to know, and of how many of those people I lost touch with. It seems that my life has always revolved around school, but I suppose everyone's at one time or another did, for school is one of the most important and most predominant parts of your life and memory. Of course, then there are those who hate school and or dropout at an early age, but still, it is an important part of one's life nonetheless.

But to my point, I've been having odd dreams about a lot of people that I have not seen or talked to since middle school and the beginning of high school. One person in particular is Cryssy, she played a very interesting role in my life, and in fact, there is an interesting story behind the way that we met.

She first appeared in my eighth grade science class, a strange child, the last of the non-conformists. She was kicked out of school very quickly though because her lifestyle choices and the way that she dressed were very much against school codes. I always found her intriguing but never thought much of it after she disappeared. Then, one day while on the phone with Jane, Cryssy suddenly was on the other line. She gave me her number and that night we talked until the next morning. For the next year, we were to spend nearly every weekend together building, destroying, shopping, and warping my mind. Her, being a person whom was forced to grow up quickly, taught me much about the world from her point of view, and also influenced me to find myself. During my freshman year, I became another of the remaining non-conformists, dyed hair, dog collar, second-hand shirts, generic raver pants, and an attitude that suited only me and was not at all stereotypical. We started losing touch about six months later, and she disappeared soon after. I later found out that she had gotten married, got her GED, and had moved away, never to be seen or heard from again.

Recently, my dreams have been about her and I have been happy while in the dreams, but saddened every time I realize that they are not real. Luckily though, I have learned to control the majority of my dreams – or at least those that take place after three A.M. – and I am able to talk to her as if we had met again after hundreds of years. Anyway though, it's times like these that I wish that I hadn't lost so many people, it hurts more than you know…I must go…Sweet dreams.

7/7 Unknown

Today was better.

I took a placebo today, I prayed. It worked, as do most placebos.

Thinking about other things helps me feel better, so after long meditation, I've discovered some things about religion.

God is based on perception and the Bible is redundant, to name a few of my problems with religion. I suppose though, that my biggest problem is not so much with God, but is more so related to his followers and the way that the Bible and God are approached.

For one, people all too often turn to God when something bad happens because they "need" him, or because they blame him. Both of these things are bad in several ways. Firstly, they don't come to him on a constant and regular basis, and as soon as they are done with him, they go on with their immoral, stupid, pointless lives. Secondly, they blame him for bad things happening, when in reality, God does neither good nor bad (these are based on perception). There are too many people in the world to make happy so why try, especially if the lot of them don't believe in you? I am more inclined to believe that God made us, then sits watching. We started screwing up, so he sent his son down to straighten us up. Here are some simple examples of that perception, Bible based, and real-life based:

Wife dies; God let my wife die! ☹
YAY! I HATED MY MOM! ☺

Planet is flooded; humanity starts over, and a lot of stupid people died ☺ A lot of people died ☹

God frees Egyptian slaves; Slaves are free! ☺ - My mistake, servants, depending on the version you read (but the Bible never changes). No one left to build my empire (think that's good? ask Pharaoh how he felt) ☹

Can't have sex, it's immoral, ☺ Sex feels good ☹; Sex feels Good ☺ Sex causes children ☹; Sex causes children ☺, Children rebel and will hate you for a long time ☹; They rebel but will learn to be adults ☺; Adults are generally stupid when not taught to be independent and disciplined AT THE SAME TIME! Etc. etc. ☹

Man is made fun of in the woods ☹, God sends a bear to eat children ☺; Children died ☹; They were rebelling so it's ok ☺

And this continues forever, but I'm sick of drawing smiley faces, therefore I conclude that religion is perception, period.

Also, religion uses guilt to get what it wants and that is simply evil because you're playing off of the emotions of lesser people. A good example is that in church they teach you that sex is bad because of the unbearable guilt you feel afterwards (among other reasons). Of course, the people that have sex all the time and don't feel guilt must obviously be evil...or is it that they just don't know they're supposed to feel guilty, so they don't. Religious nuts consider these people horrible because they have no morals, when instead they should accept the fact that, "Not everyone has the same morals as you!" Although, I do have my own morals and sentiments on sex but I'll explain them later.

This brings me to my next point, that when told to think something, the majority of people will. Just like the experiment by Mendel in the sixties, people will do things to each other when told to, despite pain and or consequences involved and or inflicted. This is apparent through the massive amounts of religious wars. It seems that the more religious someone is, the more negotiable killing becomes. This is exactly why not many people enjoy church unless they are blind to the bad things of their religion or can somehow rationalize these things to make them sound "ok." It seems that most of the religious groups are blind to their religion and don't see its obvious issues.

Furthermore, I do not believe that there is any kind of conspiracy to take over the world going on in the church because they are good people helping each other (keywords –

each other) and the brotherly love is very much appreciated and welcome – just not to me. However, I still don't like the way certain things are accomplished. For example, the way they shove their holier-than-thou attitudes in your face a lot of the time. It seems that a lot of religious people have a hard time fathoming that someone doesn't agree with them on a certain religious subject or on religion in general. In fact, I know most people would probably have a psychotic episode just from reading this. It seems they have a problem when someone questions their religion in a logical or half-truth manner. I suppose these people are insecure in their own religious beliefs (like when someone insecure with their sexuality makes fun of a gay), because if they were true to their religion and were completely secure in their knowledge, none of this should bother them.

Also, when I have a question or challenge about religion, it is met by someone repeating what they've heard, not really even knowing what it means, or in some cases is side-stepped and the person tells me to have a relationship with God. I'm sorry but I can't have a relationship with someone that I cannot at LEAST have a two-way conversation with. "Read the Bible," they say; how does that of all things help me to talk to him? I can't hear his voice and it's always the same thing; unless they want me to read another version, then I'll get new stuff completely. Heh, I can just see God up there having fun with the religions by randomly changing a few sentences in each Bible, confusing everyone. Hmm, I have to give *some* people credit though, because they are open-minded about their religion and don't feel the need to repeat themselves louder to prove me wrong and or answer simple questions.

Moreover, the idea that I could plant into myself through my sub-conscious is what will accomplish the feet of getting me through something – this is called praying. Besides, could God seriously drop money from the sky or steal all of my crack rocks away? I see this in people constantly, you can either pray and something will happen because you make it happen, or it won't because it's not humanly possible or you do not have control over the factors involved. Though, if you have strong enough will power and mind over matter going for you, by all means pray to your hearts content. I'm just saying that all too often people convince themselves of things that they startlingly accomplish on their own and then blame God, or the reverse, they don't accomplish something on their own, and they blame God. Personally, I'm more inclined to believe in the placebo effect and the law of probability mixed with human nature.

Then there are the undeniable contradictions in terms. Not in the words themselves, for I've read the Bible – parts of it – and thousands of scholars have examined and found no contradictions in words. However, I find it strange that we are not allowed to kill anyone unless they don't believe in us! Ever read Exodus? And why do we have to constantly praise someone who knows he is omniscient? God must have been neglected as a child, needs the constant reassurance and attention of his creations, and is probably really only a teenager looking for affection. I'd offer to him my services as a good listener but I have my own problems to worry about.

Then I say, that the majority of all European religions are based on the same thing and in fact, tell the same story (nearly every religion has the same story line, just in a different order and in different languages). There cannot be one ultimately correct religion because the monotheistic Middle Eastern cultures all teach in a MAJOR GENERAL WAY the same damned thing. Besides, every single religion teaches that their religion is right and everyone else's is wrong, so what gives?

Actually, I was at a sermon about other religions in my old church, and they were making-fun of Buddhism (Who'd they ever hurt!) Mormonism, and Confucianism (That's not even a religion! You can be a Confucius Christian!). They went on to be so bold as to criticize each one with no real basis in fact! They had a skit depicting Confucius as a bumbling fool and Buddha as a humming retarded monk. I happen to respect Confucius as one of the most intelligent people in the world, for I have studied him thoroughly and have found that he teaches the SAME things that Christianity teaches; the same thing goes for Buddhists. But, instead of being smart about it, they made-fun. The pastor then continued to talk about Mormonism and said that he only knew one good Mormon and that the rest were "misguided." He then told us not to be mean to them when they come to our doors, but proceeded to tell us what NOT to do, making it sound much more appealing and funny – which is what most teens would do. I have, sadly enough, seen this in Christians countless times, they make off-color jokes on the square under the guise of being cute, but in reality are just being bigots. To me, it is disgusting and I dislike it with a passion, not so much befitting that of the devil, but a passion nonetheless.

So! I conclude, that there are still things that lead me to believe that there is indeed a God, for I rarely believe in coincidences and there are too many of them in the world for me to deny an existence of some kind of divine intervention. But! As far as organized religion is concerned and the way God really is, it is to me, mans' way of rationalizing, boundarizing, and conforming to a specific sheeply way of thinking and I only trust it as far as I can throw Benny across this room. So I say with finality, that I will live my life how I see fit and I will live my life to the fullest, with the most open-mind, with the most thoughtful thoughts and feeling heart. For I know myself, I know people, I know everything, and I am God! ☺

He notices His last few sentences and wonders to Himself if they are true, save for the, "I am God" part. He repeats the words to Himself silently, thinking about each one and its meaning. He is about to continue writing when a loud sound is heard outside, causing Him to jump into a defensive stance – instinct.

Looking down He sees the scattered chunks of His semi-circle sugar-ring. With a deep breath and a confident expression, He pulls His shirt straight and steps to the edge of the sugar-ring. His confident demeanor breaks for a second and He considers returning to the corner but decides against it, for He is determined today. With a loud tone of finality He shouts, "JOOM!" steps past the bubble and moves across the room to the door…

Violence is funny.

I just realized something, I preach about how violence is bad all the time, on TV especially, and I myself am a violent person. How ironic is that?

I finally gathered up the courage to leave my bubble and went out today. I didn't want to go outside though because it is too hot, according to the orderly in the cafeteria anyway. For lunch, my first full-sized meal in a while, I had tomato soup with crackers, an apple, and water, interesting combination to say the least, however, surprisingly good. After lunch, I went back to the game room to see if Sisal was there to play a game of chess.

When I entered the room, a retarded glow befell me as everyone looked up and smiled in their own distorted way. They all had heard about what had happened and seemed somewhat concerned, but with a sharp glance knew not to say anything and quickly made their knowledge known to everyone else on the Ward. I asked Benny if he knew what had happened to Sisal and he informed me that Sisal had another violent episode when he no longer wanted to wait for me. I'm quite flattered that someone had a psychotic episode for me…How extremely funny, only *I* of all people would get a kick out of *that*, and perhaps Jane, but she's weird too so that's ok.

Sadly though, without Sisal my spirits were nearly crushed again, so I sat down in my normal spot and began to feel increasingly sorry for myself. But then I remembered that that's what I always do, and that that is always bad. So, instead, I decided to focus my mind on the people around me, to attempt to find the good in all of them, and to find the positive attitude and empathy that the doctor is always speaking of, and in fact had himself. I sat for a long while and concentrated on observing behavior and listening to thoughts, and it started to work but only slightly...

Benny is a tall, skinny, bald man around the age of thirty-eight, who looks to be in his late fifties, with orange facial hair and hazel eyes. His biggest problem is that he suffers from Delusions of Grandeur, thinking that he is Michael the archangel (there's religion again, brainwashing people!). Now, this normally would be good, but see Michael was one of God's warrior angels, so Benny, when confronted by a seemingly bad person, becomes very accusatory and often times Bible thumps the person...he hits pretty hard, I know from experience. This too does not seem too bad, but when mixed with a bit of paranoia and his Enissophobia, fear of unpardonable sin and or criticism (disorders always come in multiples), bad things begin to happen. Mostly though, he's a quiet guy unless provoked, that's when he starts sounding like a Jesus Freak, yelling and screaming about literally only God knows what. It's weird but oh well. Anyway, it seems that the only thing he likes to do is watch TV. Talking to him is like talking to a parrot sometimes, repeating what you've said questioningly and with a nervous stutter, and then answering you either incoherently or with little to no detail at all. It took me about three minutes to find out what had happened to Sisal. It's ok though, I don't plan on talking to him too too much after today, and he didn't waste my time, for I have nothing else to do.

Cole too, is an interesting character if I do say so myself. A very moody fellow with a lot to say but hardly ever out loud. He is a very paranoid person, does not trust anyone, and doesn't seem to have any emotions. In my opinion, he has great intelligence, but absolutely no encouragement or motivation to show any of it. The reason that I *know* he is intelligent though, is because of the way that he presents himself, sort of like how Forest Gump could figure out a person with their shoes, only not...ok it's nothing like that nevermind. But seriously, he's got this way about him that permeates the air around him, it screams "I AM SMART!" Besides, we can smell our own. He sits in the center of the room (this shows a dominant personality type) and watches everyone intently with a barely visible grin that subtly shouts discernment. In fact, I'm willing to bet that he knows the insides and outs of EVERYONE in this ward just because he's been sitting there for so long. I wonder what his I.Q. is...

Dear Diary:

The strange one has come back from his several days of self-imposed isolation. He's an interesting character to watch, very much dangerous though. I will definitely put more effort into figuring him out despite this danger because so far I've had more trouble than usual reading him. What bothers me the most is that he is so temperamental it's difficult to tell when he's going to be in a good mood or a fighting mood or just any mood in general.

Last week he was excited when playing chess and ping-pong with Sisal Benny and Franco but then all of a sudden he freaked out and nearly killed a man. As admirable as that quality is I hope I don't piss him off because he might attempt to kill me too which means I'll be forced to inflict large amounts of pain upon him. And as much fun as that sounds I like this place better than the rest and don't want to be shipped away to another one anytime soon.

I think I've got him pegged as a semi-normal guy and then I hear about him locking himself in a bubble of sugar? I'm not into science at all but I'm pretty sure there is no possible way for you to make a bubble out of sugar. I'm supposen I will need to talk to him figure him out, and get inside his head. Whatever, I'll figure him out from here for now.

Lieutenant Commander Cole Hartman – Out

...Oh well, I guess I'll never know because he doesn't talk, thus making it more difficult for me to "get to know him."

Mmm, I'm getting REALLY tired, so I think I'll finish this one tomorrow morning sometime, maybe after I "analyze" more people... —

It's the morning finally, I'm well rested and my belly is full, so I will continue to hone my analysis skills until maybe one day I can figure someone out better than they know themselves. Heh, wouldn't that be something, to know someone better than they know themselves when *I* hardly even know myself. Oh well. Wait, no oh well, perhaps then that should be my new goal!? Ah-ha! I've figured out what I should do now, see what sleep does for you, makes you think. Good, now what? I have no idea; maybe I'll figure myself out while figuring others out, sort of like what Jane used to do. Too bad I was too damned stubborn to really take her advice, because then maybe I'd at least know where I was headed, if I was headed in the right direction, or if I was even heading anywhere to begin with.

Jane was always talking about accepting things and about letting go of what I could not control. She told me that if I did that – among other things – I would have more control over my life and would not be so prone to anger. I never could, nor can I now, understand how letting go of things helps me to have more control. All my life I've had control of myself because I've always been aware of everything I do, not to mention what the people around me were doing. Always making sure my bases were covered and that everything was taken care of, in my opinion, is being in control of your life. But! Jane disagrees and says that I'm doing it all wrong. Unfortunately, she could never really describe it well enough for me to understand...either that or I just would never listen enough to fully understand. After almost a year of trying to get me to realize things, she just, gave-up on trying to change me, but didn't abandon me completely – thank God.

Jane is an interesting person; she has this aura about her that is somewhat intimidating to most people. Probably because her intelligence is nearly equal to my own, and at times even seems to surpass it, for she has more mental-maturity. I can't say that she was brought up differently because she has had the same problems with family as me, but has survived them better. Well, that's not true, before she found her sense of "enlightenment," she was suicidal and was a self-mutilator, whereas I decided, after being depressed a lot more often than not, that suicide was not the answer to mine or anyone else's problems. Strangely though, she was the one to figure out how to deal with family and people, so much so that she actually enjoys being with people now, despite their annoying habits. Of course, she generally uses people (not sure if it's in a good or bad way), and seems to be able to get what she wants from them by the way she talks and acts. Although, she sometimes is sarcastic and rude as well, so you can't really win with her. That's one thing, though, that I still haven't been able to figure out. I find that people are too selfish, stupid, greedy, and arrogant – which generally is misplaced – to enjoy being around, so I don't usually enjoy interacting with them.

I know recently I've wanted to, and that's because there must be something about people that I'm missing. If Jane can find so many good things in them, maybe I'm just surrounding myself with the wrong people. Sending the wrong message through my moods, facial expressions, and the way that I talk could very well be the problem. Maybe my own attitude of superiority attracts those who *think* that they are superior, but really are just self-serving, self-righteous, greedy bastards of people, looking for the next person to screw over for their own gain. So, if I portray an interest in such people, then I need to change it, because it really is annoying.

How though? I am an intelligent person that is pissed off at the world, how do I stop myself from doing that? Empathy? Positive attitude? These seem to be the two things that I keep coming back to. But I don't know how to show them! This is so frustrating! I KNOW what I need to do,

"but I have no idea how to do it! What the hell does everyone want from me!? A complete change of my entire life and personality!?" He shouts to Doctor Shutz.

"It's not what we want from you, it's what you need from yourself. We do not control you – even though you seem to let us – you control yourself. But living in here should not be something you are content with, it does nothing but set you back and help you to hold on to the things of your past. It seems that almost every session has been based on your past and what has happened then, hardly the now, and certainly never the later. You need to let go of these things and move on with your life." Sighing, Doctor Shutz waits for a response.

"But that's difficult, the past is what defines who I am! Am I supposed to just get rid of all of that and start over!?"

"No...and yes. Eh...it's hard, you need to hold on to the things that have helped you, not hindered you. You hold on to the most negative memories you can find as a way to continue your crusade against stupid, mean, fake people. You can't keep generalizing and stereotyping every person you come across, it's not healthy and it's what prevents you from doing a lot of things."

Hopelessly, "But, I don't think I've ever met anyone that wasn't stupid or mean or fake."

"Yes you have! What about Jane, Isaac, Frank, Me, your...all of those people! Don't they count for anything? Or are they stupid too?"

"Well they're different..."

"And there are a LOT of people like that out there, you just don't want to see them. Why is it that you keep yourself in a bubble, away from everyone else, unable to see anything good in the world?"

"I...I don't know! Maybe because I'm afraid!"

"Afraid of what?"   Doctor Shutz says hopefully, possibly getting somewhere.

"Of people! They're just so difficult! So many rules and things that you can do to upset them! We all know I can't figure people out like you can, so I don't even really try! In the end someone always gets hurt and that person is usually me!"

"Then how did you find Jane and the others? Didn't you have to figure them out? Why aren't they difficult?"

"With them it was simple, they basically gave me all of the answers. They were the only ones to be forthright with their feelings, personalities, and other what not. They made me want to like them, so I did, and now they're my best friends. But all I have is them and perhaps a few others, I have no 'friends,' or 'acquaintances,' or anything like that, but that's what I want!"

"There you go then."

"There I go what?"

"You do want more than just them, and that's good, that's wonderful in fact. And you can have more, because there are more of those kinds of people out there in the world. However difficult to find, but there nonetheless."

"Rrrr! That's the problem, what if I don't find them!? What if they don't find me? How do I go about doing all of that 'interaction' junk?"

"You will find them because there are a lot more good people in the world then you give credit for. If you just started at least looking more approachable, then perhaps you would have an easier time finding them or visa versa."

"How am I not approachable?"

"*Whenever I see you, you have this look of disdain and resentment. When people see that they become intimidated and afraid to a point where introducing themselves, let alone forming a long lasting relationship, seems frightening and impossible.*"

"*Oh...yeah I noticed that the other day too...*" He trails off, thinking for a moment, "*What did you mean by, 'Even though you seem to let us,' when you were talking about me and control.*"

"*I said what?*"

"*You said something like, 'We don't control you, even though you seem to let us.' What does that mean?*"

"*Oh. Umm, I mean that you always seem to base your moods on everyone else and everything that's going on around you instead of controlling your moods. It's part of your instability.*"

"*I do? Can you give me an example, so I know exactly what you're talking about?*"

"*Sure...Umm, ok like when your friends were here you were ecstatic and hyper the whole day, but that wore off after a while and you were angry and depressed again. Then when your...umm...father died...you isolated yourself from everyone instead of facing it head on. You let things affect you too much whether it be in a good or bad way.*"

"*Oh. Well isn't that normal?*"

"*Those are kind of bad examples because those are two big things, but you know what I mean right? You do that a lot, even with things that shouldn't bother you. Too many people base their lives off of everything else around them: relationships, money, a job, and things of this nature. What you should do is be stable, try to keep yourself at a certain, 'level' if you will, so that you're not always swinging back 'n' forth with your moods.*"

"*Why is it so bad to let things like that bother you?*"

"*It's not that it's bad, it's just unhealthy. Mood swings like that can cause stress and we all know how you react to stress.*"

He interrupts with a chortle, "*Yes we do.*"

"*Yah,*" continues Doctor Shutz, "*but we all know how you react to stress and it's not good at all. Also there's the physical aspect; mood swings change your eating habits, brain chemistry,*" *sleeping habits, and overall body functions, either indirectly or directly. Don't you notice that when you're in a good mood you'll eat more, get more sleep, and sometimes even have enough energy to run? But when you're in a bad mood, you sleep at odd hours of the day, don't eat, are lethargic, and just don't care about anything in general. Sure being moody is natural, but I think all people, including you, should at least try to stabilize their moods, if not for health, but because it makes life more enjoyable."*

"Ah. I see..."

"Good, I'm glad. Do you have any questions? Our time is nearly up for today."

"Yah, how do I do all that stuff?"

"By giving everyone a chance and by finding a way to stabilize yourself."

"I can do the first part, what about the second part?"

"I can't give you all the answers you know, you should figure some of this stuff out on your own. Besides, it's different for everyone"

"Can you at least point me in the right direction?"

The Doctor sighs, "The best thing I can think of is for you to find something stable to keep your moods 'level,' instead of allowing all these variables in your life, like other people, or time of day etceteras, to effect you."

"I think I get it..."

I must surround myself with good people by being a good person myself. That way I will stop generalizing, and in the process have the type of relationships I want. Only then will I be able to figure myself out and accomplish the goal of being stable, and in the process, get the hell out of here! Now, to put all of this into action...that's easier said than done.

But today's been long, so I won't do it now, in fact, I think I'll retire to my room to meditate on my new ideas. Thoughtful Day.

7/11 8:22 p.m.

4
Interaction

I'm getting better.

It's been over a month since I last wrote in my journal. This is a good thing. For, a lot has happened, and the only reason I feel the need to write is for future references. My journal is to help calm me down, and for the past month, I have been rather calm; to the point, at least, that I haven't gotten into trouble, and that I've been able to think clearly.

Recently, I've been "hanging-out" with the other guys like I was before. Mostly playing games, taking walks, talking about inane philosophy (mostly for my entertainment), and watching a bit of TV and or movies that are still stimulating to the mind. These things, as well as others, have been keeping me busy and I am slowly learning how to interact with people again, despite their somewhat undesirable idiosyncrasies. In fact, I've actually learned to like a lot more of the people here than I ever thought possible.

Take for example Cole, I found him to be a quiet, seemingly cold person when I first saw him. But now, after a month of pestering and semi-encouragement, I've actually gotten him to talk to me a bit. According to Dr. Shutz, Cole does not speak to anyone, so for some reason I must have triggered something in him, because now we're *almost* friends – as far as a semi-catatonic goes. As it turns out, Cole is even an interesting guy; he is an Army veteran and was a soldier during the last war. He suffers from post traumatic stress disorder, paranoia, and generally mistrusts the whole world and the people in it. This is because his CO deserted him during some important mission, and on his way back to base, saw horrible sights from a bombed village. That, mixed with about thirty years of service and other such things, has seriously scarred him for life. He has lived in several different institutions throughout the past eight years and was finally stuck here about two months ago because the freedom and care that this place gives to its patients. He seems to like it.

So far, we've talked a lot about the wars, and about sports. He is a very wise person because of his age and experience and I admire him. He's taught me that respect and acceptance for everyone including yourself are most important. Confidence, he explained, comes from the knowledge that you are as good as you can be or want to be, not from what other people think you are. One of my biggest problems, it seems, is that I base my self-worth off of what other people think of me; Cole and Dr. Shutz both say that that's bad. So far, I agree with him, and am actively in the process of realizing myself and changing the things that I don't like. However, I believe that the changing process, is what will take the longest.

He said that he once had a dream to compete in Olympic Wrestling – I find that exciting. He is from Ohio, and that gives him a major advantage because apparently you can start wrestling in fifth grade and continue on through to college – that's what he did. The only reason that he didn't compete, though, is because he was drafted when America started losing the wars. He said that wrestling and track were the only two sports that he respected. Luckily, I was a track star in high school (long distance running), and in fact won a few medals, but never competed in anything bigger than JV Championships.

Anyway, it seems that Cole is beginning to trust me, for he has revealed certain said secrets to me, that I won't even write here. It looks as though we are helping each other out, in a sort of symbiotic relationship. In fact, I've even gotten him to start interacting, and we've both been smiling more often than not to say the least. My hope is that with his help and with Dr. Shutz's help, as well as others', I can get out of here sooner than later. I don't want to abandon anyone, it's just that I've been in here for nearly four years and I'm ready to get out. For, I am finally setting goals (which Cole and the Doc also say are important), and I want to accomplish those goals. Maybe I'll write those tomorrow, or at least what I've come up with so far. It looks like Cole has been playing a more important part in my life than I thought he or anyone else in here ever would.

Oh ah! I almost forgot, as I thought, some terrorist got a hold of anti-matter, and are now making threats to EVERY country that doesn't fall to their demands. I don't remember exactly what they wanted, but I'm sure that it has something to do with either money or power or both. Luckily for me though, I don't live on the eastern seaboard so I couldn't care less about what happens. Actually, that's not true, I *do* care, but I'm not afraid or anything like that, because it would be a shame if a large amount of people died for no good God reason. But! That is the price of human nature is it not? Yes, yes it is, human nature is the horrid thing that keeps us from evolving, but we all already know that, besides, I'm supposed to be looking *past* human nature. For, on the individual level, people cannot be generalized by the slightest; this, I have recently found out through my new "friend."

As far as this past month goes, Dr. Shutz is very pleased. It seems too, that he is pleased with his own abilities as a Doctor, for he is one of the few doctors to "cure" more than one person. This is strange because the point of therapy is almost never to cure anyone, but it seems that Dr. Shutz is on a crusade to do so. Either way, I find it rather funny to see how excited he gets when I speak positively about my day or my thoughts etc. In fact, he says that if I am genuine in my attitude, and if I continue on my path of learning how to cope with things, that I might very well be on my way to getting out of here. Each time he says that, though, he emphasizes that, if I do get out, I should continue to grow in every way possible.

In short, that's been my month. So I will retire, and write, maybe, tomorrow. Good Month.

8/14 2:32 p.m.

My goals.

So far, I've come up with some general future goals, but nothing too specific because most of these depend on what happens next. Also, they depend on each other, because if one doesn't happen, the rest won't; they all lead into each other like a chain of logic.

First, foremost, and most obviously, I would like to get the hell out of here. I used to hate this place, but was content in the fact that I had to do nothing and therefore felt no need to leave. Recently though, I've become restless in that I finally want to do something with my life. It seems as though I actually have some kind of motivation to get out and experience the world, despite its insidious nature. Who'd of thunk it?

Next, I would like to complete my high school education and then possibly a college education. Luckily, I will only have to complete a year and a half worth of credits, which can easily be accomplished through home school, night school, or some other inexpensive education. Any of these will be extraordinarily simple and I should have no problem earning nine credits. After that, with my intelligence level, I should definitely go to college and attempt to find a career. As far as a major though, I have no idea what I should do. I could probably start a career in anything ranging from music, to computers, to psychology, or even teaching. So, I'll wait until I decide what will be best for me, have the most fun with, and what I will be most helpful to. Luckily, I couldn't care less about money, as long as I have a place to live and am content with how I live there I'll be fine. After I have my education and a career, I should be set, so that brings me to my next set of goals.

Recently, I've found that relationships are more important to me than I usually let myself care to believe. So, during the aforementioned I will also get back in touch with all or as many of my friends from high school who are still in town. Then, I will try as hard as possible to forge new relationships and strengthen old ones. Sounds simple enough, but will probably be one of the bigger, more difficult goals to accomplish; balancing between school, friends, and whatever else.

Anyway, I think that's about all of the goals I have for now. A lot of the others, if there are any, are more so mini-goals based off of the bigger ones. They are mostly about who I'm going to get in touch with, or what classes I have to take to get my GED. But it looks like it's time for lunch, so I'm going to go eat a chicken sandwich and play a game of Chess with Sisal, he misses me. Good day.

8/15 11:50 a.m.

I am alone.

As I sit here, I realize how alone in the world I am right now. Sure I have my newest friends, but they are not deep friends capable of supporting me. Not to worry myself, I am not backsliding, I am just thinking.

So much has happened recently that's it seems almost like a dream. I mean, what was preventing me from moving forward the first few years that I was here? Was I too stubborn, not ready to get out, was God teaching me something? Who knows, I don't think I do or ever will. But that's neither here nor there, because the point is I seem to have finally come to terms and am now in the midst of fixing my problems. In fact, Dr. Shutz has even lowered my drug dosage again, and still I have been able to keep control of myself. But again, I don't have too many problems while I'm in the protected walls of this hospital, so it's hard to gauge whether or not the drugs, my own solutions, or my surroundings are what help me. Hopefully, when I do eventually get out, things won't be as hard as they used to be, and if they are, my true friends will be the ones to help me through it...It seems that everything is based off of friends isn't it?

Oh well, I guess I will soon find out, for according to the Doc, I will be out of here shortly. Until then, I will continue my "crusade" against my own bad behavior and fanatical thoughts. Until the end, Good Day!

8/15 10:50 p.m.

Today was fun.

The hospital has come upon a large sum of money from an anonymous contributor. To say the least, the guy was generous, and now the hospital is even better equipped than it was before. In the interest of boosting moral, though, they spent a sizeable sum of that money on a concert for the patients. The band, "As Far As We Can," is not a well-known band, but no one really cared, and as far as I could tell, everyone had fun.

All five wards were there, including those who require restraints. Benny, Sisal, Cole, Frank, Wilson, and I all sat together because we consider ourselves the most stable people – birds of a feather, flock together. At first, no one seemed to be impressed by the "New Age Ska" band, which was expected because their lyrics were made more so for teenagers, not paranoids, compulsives, and narcissists. However, much to my surprise, the schizoids were the first ones to "get into it." They began dancing much like "white boys," with absolutely no rhythm and by mostly shaking their hips. Though, for unusually asocial people, they seemed to have some kind of emotion in their movement.

Soon, the entire room was catching on to the erratic rhythm of the schizoids, and everyone began rising to their feet to "dance." My group, being that of the more stiff variety, was seemingly content in their chairs...for a while. In fact, it took the majority of the band's set, but finally, when a song called "I'm so Happy" came on, we all jumped to our feet to yell and dance like fools. We all jumped around to a song about a man's strange day and how it was comfy cozy and oh so fun. Heh, I even saw Cole stand up for a few moments to jump and hoot about the happy man in the song. In fact, I think I even heard him singing along with chorus – "I'm so happy! Feelin' sappy! My life is rockin'! I'm feelin' super sockin'! There'll be no sorrow! When I wake-up tomorrow!" Actually, come to think of it, by the end of the song nearly everyone was singing along. But that's when the sad part came. ☹ They sang a song about a fallen love life, and it was so well written (better than any poem I could write), that they had even the coldest souls in the room about ready to cry...I hope the story wasn't true though, because what that guy went through was harsh. Oh well, glad it's not me. ☺

Finally, after about an hour, they were ready to play the last song. *Everyone* in the room was standing in anticipation of the great finale. It started with a long, high-pitched guitar blast that echoed throughout the room with wonderful electronic resonance. Then, all at once the "ska kids" jumped into the air and played one of the best songs I have ever heard. This song seemed to mix the complex melody and cadence of a famous orchestra with the imaginative ideals of ska kids with a purpose. All at once, everyone in the room, including the orderlies, felt the compulsive need to jump in place, bang their heads, and scream! This song evoked the most profound thoughts and emotions I've had in a very long time; so deep, that I can't even begin to explain these thoughts and feelings to myself, let alone do them justice on paper. So, I will describe it in the only way I know how, with the title, "As Far As We Can."

At the end of the song, everyone, including Cole, was screaming for more, but we were unfortunately met with disappointment as the band said they had no more songs to play. Despite the lack of encore, everyone's satisfaction was more than obvious in one way or another and I think that the band was pleased to be appreciated. As everyone filed out of the room, it seemed almost anti-climactic as we all returned to our prior moods. Everyone, is a strong word, for I believe that most of us got something out of the concert other than just music. It looks as though the moral booster was a success, at least for me because everyone was raving about the concert afterwards. But I'm off to bed, jumping around drains you quickly – Awesome Night.

8/16 9:58 p.m.

I field trip gone awry.

Today several of the patients and I were taken to Quiggly's to buy things with our monthly allowance of six dollars. I personally do not buy much and have saved up nearly sixty dollars so that I can buy a laser trimmer, for I have decided to re-grow my beard.

It was interesting, for the fact that I usually decide not to participate in the monthly shopping trip, I have not been to Quiggly's for a very long time. While walking through the aisles I remembered all of the times that I used to run around pulling random things off of the shelves only to throw them or place them somewhere else on the opposite side of the store. I bet that I've pissed off a large number of stock boys by making them fix the canned food mountains, broken shelves, replace missing items, and clean up all of the messes that I've made. I'm glad I was never an aisle cleaner or courtesy clerk. A stock boy is a simpler job, I never had to clean up or fix things, just fill shelves. Of course, this was not the best part of the trip. No, the best part was when Robert turned up missing.

All of us were herded into the van with one chaperone, as the rest of the babysitters looked for Robert. During that hour, the store was searched top to bottom, every single office and backroom was looked in and then locked. Several of the store workers searched the parking lot but no one could find Robert. Duncan and the rest of them decided not to call the institution because it would create unnecessary panic, paperwork, and reprimands.

Robert is a quiet, paranoid, and phobic person. I don't know his actual diagnosis, but I know that he spends most of his time watching everyone with wide eyes (he rarely blinks and is given eye drops regularly). He sits in the corner of whatever room he is put into, twitching madly, and mumbling to himself strange incoherent things. Normally, people like him would not be on my ward, but because of his strange nature and occasional outbursts of emotion – no emotion in particular – he is admitted with the rest of the aggravated people. Anyway though, he is normally quiet and unnoticeable to the point that he is generally unseen – being short and with plain features does not help this – making it more difficult for anyone to find him, especially in a large department store.

After nearly an hour of searching, our chaperones were ready to give up and call the police, when suddenly, George found Robert. One of the obsessive-compulsive patients was beginning to grow uneasy and needed to pee. Strangely, after George mentioned having to pee, several others, including me, needed to as well, so we were taken to the bathroom. On our way out of the bathroom, George began fixing everything in the aisles, including an oddly arranged row of toilet paper packages. In fact, he seemed so dissatisfied with the way that they were arranged on the shelf, he decided to take down the entire shelf and restock them himself. At first, we attempted to stop him but he would not stop until his compulsion was fulfilled. We ignored him until there was a strange whimpering sound. We all stared as something was revealed behind the toilet paper. As we looked on, our creeping suspicions were confirmed, because there was Robert, curled up in a ball, mumbling to himself and twitching on the bottom shelf of a Quiggly's toilet paper aisle.

Anyway, that was the highlight of the day, so I think I'll go play a game or be bored or make myself busy in one way or another. Good day.

8/18 6:44 p.m.

I am leaving. (*He looks at the opening to what could be the last entry He will ever write inside His home of three and a half years. A feeling of warmth, hope, nostalgia, and overall uneasiness rushes through Him, turning His stomach into a pit of ice.*)

It seems that Dr. Shutz thinks that I will be ready to leave very soon. It's been a week since my last entry again, and even in that short time, I have made slow but noticeable progress. My attitudes have changed only slightly since my goal setting, semi-revelations, and the concert, and have changed vastly since the beginning of this journal. Surely though, I have many more steps to take in the real world, but I am now sure that I am at least prepared and capable of handling some of the real world.

Strangely though, I thought that I would be more excited about leaving, but perhaps that is because I have made friends recently that I do not particularly want to leave. Luckily though, the relationships that I have forged here are more so strong acquaintances, and in only one instance, a good friend – Cole. For the past few months, he has helped me a great deal more than I thought possible. His wisdom and experiences have proved to be a great tool in my evolution, and will prove to be a source of help in the future I'm sure. The few things that he has said to me, seem to have helped more than anything else, for it seems that he is enlightened in his own special militaristic sort of way. Also, it seems that he has been able to find and point out certain characteristics about me that I might never have found on my own and for that I thank him. He is one quiet, paranoid person that I *will* miss greatly…perhaps I should tell him these things in person.

Anyway, I will also miss the rambling rhythms of the not so coherent schizophrenics, and the wandering cadence of the OCD patients, for they are what have made this trip more bearable, in the most frightening way possible. For, without them as a distraction, I probably would have killed myself with my own thoughts and or just killed myself.

It's strange, suddenly my entire stay here, seems unusually short, almost as if I've only just gotten here, but just the other month it seemed like an eternity. Neat how perception works isn't it? Yes well, it is all quite neat, and it is all perception, so I shouldn't be surprised. Nonetheless, I am ready to move on, and am also scared of what will happen next. For, when I finally get out, what am I to do? Where am I to go? Will people let me back into their lives? Will my problems start over or will I fix them?…So many variables…perhaps I should learn to control these variables. In time I will I suppose, I mustn't rush things, I'm betting that my first few weeks will be awkward to say the least.

Well, I have an evaluation with the five head psychologists (all of different schools if I remember correctly), and that will determine what will happen to me. If they let me go, then I'll be out by the end of this week, and if not, then I'll stay in for another long period of time, only to have an evaluation again if Dr. Shutz deems me ready.

Depending on what happens tomorrow, depends if I write…Good Night.

8/24/10 8:45 p.m.

Upon entering the examination room, several men in white coats greet Him from around a U-shaped table in the center of the room. There are chairs for an audience but none of the chairs are filled. He is asked to sit and does so in a nervous, untrusting manner. After confirming file information and dispensing with formalities, each doctor takes his turn asking questions.

"It says here that you were admitted into this hospital on twelve, twenty three, two thousand six. Why is it that you have remained with us for so long?" asks one of the head doctors.

"I've been here so long because I never felt it necessary to change myself."

"And how have you changed yourself recently? Why do you think you're ready to leave us?" the doctor asks incredulously.

"Please stop asking more than one question at a time," He says, somewhat annoyed.

"Sorry. How have you changed?"

"I haven't changed one hundred percent of course, because I am not really exposed to something that can change me. However, I was recently visited by my friends and that renewed my non-existent motivation to better myself. Also, I've been talking to Cole Hartman

a lot and he has given me a lot of advice as far as dealing with life and other such life-obstacles."

"Don't you think your sudden change is...well, a little too sudden. It seems as if you've done a complete one-eighty overnight."

"Trust me sir, I know that I have far to go, but I believe that I am at least suitable for reality. Keeping me here is not going to make me better, it is only going to keep me at a certain level and I will never really grow."

Another doctor interrupts, "I'm sorry, did you say, 'suitable for reality?'"

"Yes, why, is that bad or something?" He asks, puzzled at the questions.

"Ah, what do you think reality is?" The doctor asks childishly.

He rolls His eyes, "Is this what you do? Nit-pick my words? I know what the word 'reality' means and I know that this here is real. I do not consider it 'reality' because I am exposed to nothing that happens in the 'real' world. I am sheltered and surrounded with people with the same problems as me. It would be like calling public school, public. You are not in public while in school because you are surrounded by similar people that are subjected to the same thing that you are, so don't placate me."

"You seem hostile, why should we let you go?"

Simply, "You seem hostile as well. Lighten up and I will too."

The doctors all look at each other questioningly, then realize that they are perhaps being childish, and rethink their approach. "Alright, you seem intelligent and sound like you've thought things out, why don't you tell us your plan and or ideas for after you leave," says another doctor.

"Thank you. My plan is to further my self-teaching of control and to continue to listen to the advice and wisdom of people older than I and of people that have been through the same things that I've been through. Granted I'm not perfect and granted I'm still somewhat aggressive, I believe that I have changed enough that it would be better for you, meaning the hospital, and me, to leave. I — "
He is interrupted:

"How is it better for us?" asks the warden.

Sighing He continues, "Listen please," the warden nods apologetically, "It is better for you financially because all I do is take up space, eat your food, take your allowances, and cost you other living expenses. Also, with the huge amount of people with worse problems than me piling up in here, I am not really on the top of the list anymore. I seem to be able to handle myself well enough for society's standards, and I also want out."

The doctors all think for a second, and one of them thinks of another question, "What do you plan on doing after you leave? Would you like to be placed into one of our De-instutional Homes?"

"No thanks, I actually plan on finding my old friends Isaac and Frank, whom recently visited and said that they could provide me with a place to live – with them."

The doctors look to Shutz and Shutz nods His head, vouching for Isaac and Frank's words and actual existence.

"Furthermore, I would like to finish my high school education and perhaps make enough money with whatever job I land, to start a college career."

"That's good, you answered my other two questions about money and education. Let me think…does anyone else have any other questions?"

One of the more skeptical doctors spoke up, "I see no evidence leading me to believe that you would be able to survive for even a minute out there! The world is very different now than it was when you first came to us. It is corrupt, dirty, and filled with horrible people, what makes you think you can really survive it!?"

"Because I have my friends to help me, and will find the good people amongst the bad."

"I don't think you have the ability nor the gumption to last two seconds outside of here," he says snidely, "In fact, I'm willing to bet that you'll end up right back here within a short time, ranting and raving and carrying on about only God knows what! I bet you can't take pressure of any kind. I don't even believe you've changed, you're just the same damned person you were when you first walked in here, only now you think you're better and you're really not!" Several of *the doctors looked at him questioningly, but were ignored, realizing his technique.*

After thinking about these comments He squints at the doctor and glances at the rest of them, all who seem strangely ok with what has just been said. With intense calm, "Hmm. Well...I'm sorry you're such a closed-minded professional that feels the need to push my buttons to prove a point. I'll tell you something, in my mind I feel that I have changed enough to realize when someone is being an asshole, and I believe that right now you are. In fact, I'll tell you all right now, that I am just as professional as you all are, and I know when and when not to have sudden outbursts, and now is not the time. I suppose none of us will really ever know if I'm truly different or not will we? But, since I know the difference between right and wrong, and I also know enough to control myself in front of a room full of people that are to decide my fate, I will remain quiet and content in my own ability to accept the opinion of one doctor without overreacting."

They all look at Him not knowing what to say, do, or feel, for He has just said something that makes so much sense in an unexpected way, that it is difficult to judge whether or not He is dangerously crazy, or frighteningly sane. Several moments pass and finally none of them have anything left to say and the review is adjourned so that all of the doctors have time to review the case and make their final decisions.

Part 2

5
New Beginnings

Dear Dr. Shutz,

It seems that it is finally my time to leave this hospital and it's your fault! Thank you, for without your help I would not have ever been able to "recover." I understand that I have much farther to go, but with your true wisdom and "emotional positive regard," I've taken the first steps in the journey to sanity. I regret though, of course, that it took me so long, and that I was so stubborn in the beginning. I apologize for that because I now realize that being an asshole, to you especially, is neither productive nor good for mine or anyone else's health. It seems that I am the second person you can put on your "cured" list. But then again perhaps not, because are *any* of us ever cured? I mean, aren't we *all* a bit crazy to a greater or lesser extent? It seems so, just that some of us get caught, and some of us are more socially acceptable than the rest.

Anyway, you've been a great friend to me to say the least and I could never really do it justice on paper or in person for that matter, so you'll have to take my word for it. But I will try. I was once told that people come into each other's lives for reasons, seasons, or forever. You were in my life for a reason, which turned into a season, which I'm glad is not forever. ☺ You're a great man, you have a lot of wisdom, and you should be proud of yourself for being able to help so many people, even those of us who are, "hopeless," or are catatonic. I will remember you and your words always, and you will always be loved in that platonic, patient-doctor sort of way. Wish me luck on my journeys through life, and try not to forget your four-year patient that just didn't know when to shut the hell up. Perhaps one day I'll see you again – outside of work, but until then, Good life!

Your not-so-crazy friend,
(Unreadable signature)

I am free today!

Hahaha! I am no longer trapped in the confines of that frighteningly sterile room or hospital! I think that perhaps I will go home now. Wait no, home is bad, I'll go find my old friends, maybe they'll let me stay with them for a while.

For the record, my release was a momentous occasion. My evaluation went smoothly and I seemed to have answered every question to the satisfaction of the doctors and warden. Upon packing my things and leaving, I was met by just about every patient on the ward that I had ever seen and or talked to during the course of the years. It seems that every one of them took some kind of liking and or interest in me because of my strange mysterious nature. Apparently, my behavior towards the end even inspired a few other people to do the same thing – get better. It's strange, I never thought that it would be possible for me of all people, to inspire someone to be a better person, but it looks like I have. I guess when you figure things out and make it known, others catch on to it and do the same thing. In a sad sort of way I regret causing people to copy me in such a sheeply manner, but on the other side, I'm glad that it was for a good cause and not violence or religion related.

Cole especially seemed sad in his professional, military way. His eyes were downcast and his posture was slightly different than normal, but was not a slouch. He looked at me proudly, but angrily, for I think he was beginning to like me. I say that only because lately his tone was that of curiosity instead of irritated appeasement. Also, upon leaving, he stood at attention and saluted me, but then again, he probably does that to everyone that annoys him and has never been in the military right? ☺...He will not be someone I forget easily.

Also, Sisal and I decided that, for old time's sake, we would play one more game of chess. I don't remember who won because it was not really important. What was important was that Sisal and I taught each other how to interact. It was nice, when I stood up to leave and shake his hand, he wrapped his large arms around me, squeezed as hard as he could, and began crying on my shoulder. At first, I stiffened, but soon felt the need to hug him as well, so I did. He too, will be someone that I will not forget easily. I hope to visit them someday as a visitor, not a patient.

Anyway, I finally left after saying bye to several other people, and the regret and sadness that I felt earlier about leaving everyone seemed to disappear completely, because for the first time in four years I am able and allowed to do *anything* that I want (within lawful reason). In fact, I feel that one large weight has been lifted from my shoulders and suddenly millions of doors are opened in my path – sounds corny I know, but true nonetheless.

So now, I need to find out where Isaac lives, hopefully his parents will have an address or phone number. Right now, I'm on a bus to the city, hoping that my first serious day out will end uneventfully. I have with me my pills, a small duffel bag of civilian clothing, my musical keypad, my wallet filled with cards, pictures, and money (very little), and my dignity. I hope that Isaac and Frank will help me restart my life and let me stay with them for a while, in fact I hope that a lot of my friends will do that. Of course, that might put them out a great deal, especially since they are only as old as I am, and could possibly be having troubles themselves. Oh well, I'm a freeloader by nature so it never hurts to try.

Meanwhile, a lot of people are looking at me quite queerly, you'd think they've never seen anyone write before. Well, I have been told that when I write I look very absorbed in what I'm doing, they must think I'm writing a book or something. Oh well, who cares, I don't think I ever could, I'm not organized enough, plus my writing isn't that good, but that's got nothing to do with the price of gas, I'm out on my own and that's all that matters!

(He puts His pen down for a moment to search the outside world, recognizing and remembering the things and places that He sees. Moments turn to minutes as He is enthralled by the memories of places visited and the possibilities of those places He has never seen before. He almost misses His stop, but at the last minute pulls the cord and runs to the bus's exit, then walks the six blocks to Isaac's old house.)

Heh, I'm actually sitting on Isaac's front steps, nervously wondering if I should knock or run. SO! In order to calm my nerves I will rationalize the situation.

Let's see, I have known his family since first grade and even though I never really talked to them all that much, they all know me and used to welcome me whenever I came over – announced or unannounced. Also, despite my annoying habit of eating all of their food and drinking all of their drink, they still took care of me when I needed them to, and also took me in for a few days when I ran away from home (we lived only a few blocks away). Also, they're nice people, and I'm only looking for Isaac, it's not like I'm asking them to buy me a house or even take me in for a few days, so who cares, I'm knocking. *(He closes His notebook without ending the entry, tucks it under His arm, and walks to the door. After slight hesitation, He knocks three times and, as always in the past, the sound of Isaac's dog running towards the door barking is heard.)*

Settling in.

It turns out that Isaac and Frank live together in a North side apartment just like we had always planned. Ironically too, I am living with them now as well. So, it seems that things are in order as they should be, for now, and it is time for me to make mini-goals. I'm not going to write them down like I did before because I'm tired for one, there are too many of them, and it really doesn't matter because I'm in the process of creating, and completing the lot of them currently.

Among the more important ones though, is my job search. I have limited experience in the job world, but am good at many unintelligible tasks that could get me a part or full-time job at pretty much anywhere that pays minimum wage. So, I've applied to about a million places within the last two weeks and have been calling each one of them periodically, hoping for an interview. So far not so good, but I have hope.

Also, in the interest of furthering my job options I've been looking into going back to school. I am too old for high school, but am just right for community college. So, in the interest of finishing my GED and possibly going to one college or another, I've been doing a lot of Internet research. It's amazing the kind of stuff you can find, and how fast you can find it these days. I remember my computer was the cream of the crop when it had four gigabytes of hard drive space. But now! Isaac and Frank have jointly invested in a computer with one hundred twenty-two giga*quads* of hard drive space and some insanely large amount of RAM! Their computer thinks faster than I do for God's sake! Also, the majority of their computer's self-communication hardware is made with optical chips. They work the same as the old CDs, by with reflecting light, but are much more efficient, and can hold at least ten times the information. The guys also tell me about new neural processing units that are actual bits of brain tissue extracted from newly dead people that are then grown in labs and somehow incorporated into the computers CPU. I don't know how exactly it works and supposedly is still very expensive, but it's quite awesome nonetheless. But oh well, who cares, what we have gets me the information I need ASAP and with no problems – nothing like my old computer. So anyway, I've found out that I can take all the classes I missed in high school, and also take some college prep courses. Then, depending on my money situation and what I want to major in, depends on if I'll go to college, but that's something to stress out about later.

But enough about me, let's talk about you. Anyway, I think that's it for today, I'll write about my job (if I get one) and how I'm doing as far as backsliding later when I'm not dying of boredom and sleep deprivation. Good night!

8/29 12:16 a.m.

My nights.

For the last two days, it has been difficult for me to sleep here. There is dead silence through the night, which you would think would make it easier for me to sleep, but in fact has made it harder. The only sound I here on a random basis is that of the people next door and or the slight breeze rustling the trees. I lay on my back, fully clothed, trying to sleep, and am not yet able to get comfortable, of course, that could be because I'm on the pull out, but I doubt that that's got anything to do with it. Strangely though, I find that I am able to sleep better if I lay on the floor. I don't think it has anything to do with confidence because while on the floor I can hear vibrations and clicks and other sounds from the various appliances and machines that are scattered throughout the building and inside its walls and floors. It's strange, I never noticed this need for sound before, but I guess that's because I grew accustomed to it over the years and in fact enjoyed it to a certain extent. I suppose it has something to do with my fear of being completely alone. Sure I enjoy *my* time every once in a while, but that's usually when I'm awake and there are people within earshot incase I happen to freak out about something. Also, I am less afraid of the sunlight than I am of the dark. It's stupid I know, newly an adult and I'm still somewhat afraid of the dark. Oh well, I suppose everyone is actually afraid of the dark, except those whom thrive in the dark, feeding off of the innocent, making their deals and participating in their illegal activities. The dark, especially in larger cities, is where rapes, prostitution, illegal gambling, and where drug transactions used to happen. Now of course, most drugs are no longer illegal, because it's just a smarter solution than the "War against Drugs" ever was. It's funny how people will do something *more* if they're not supposed to. The whole risk and appeal of getting caught, like having sex in public, or better yet, when your parents are home. It seems so exciting and different and "it must be good because it's supposed to be bad." Funny how, when softcore drugs were legalized, people slowly stopped caring. Now, petty crime has been somewhat taken care of and is no longer a problem. Of course, that was then replaced with political hate crimes between the fundamentalists, naturalists, conservationists, separatists, and all of the -ists you can think of. They all started out with their signs and opinions, picketing places and or people and or government policies that did not agree with them. But of course, those people were, unheard, so those unheard people decided that they would make more noise. So, like nearly every group in history that was or is obsessed and convinced of their own opinions, violence started, hate crimes and all of the destruction related things you can think of were committed. Riots broke out in several of the major cities; Chicago, LA, New

York, and more, and Marshal Law was declared in the majority of them. To this day, nothing has really been the same. It reminds me of the Civil War, friends and family members turning against each other because each believes in a different – ists movement. Many people were killed during these riots and the "factions," have turned into modern day gangs, killing each other on the streets and refusing to work or be seen together in public. The president and the rest of the bureaucrats in D.C. have their hands tied and are unable to influence or enforce the remainder of the dwindling problem – for the new "Civil War" has become boring to the majority of the people – because most everyone blames the *government* instead of *themselves*. It's asinine, but who really cares, I live in a small enough town that everyone knows and or loves each other – lucky me. Heh, 'who really cares,' that's this countries new slogan. Apathy has taken over everything and that is why nothing really works anymore. Of course, it could just be the legalized drugs…

Wow, all of that rambling has actually gotten me tired, especially since I was only trying to write about my inability to sleep. So, it worked, perhaps I'll do this more. Short night.

8/31 5:08 a.m.

Strangers.

I have been somewhat uncomfortable around many of the strangers that the guys have had me meet within the last few days. It seems that they've made a lot more friends in the time that's passed than I thought they ever could. Their friends are nice and seemingly good people but they insist on touching me a lot more than I am comfortable with. Also, they are loud and insistent on asking me questions about my life in the institution. At this time, I really don't have much to say and probably won't ever really have too much to say about it because it was a very simple, boring, uneventful time in my life. I am now beginning to regret it and have already forgotten most of what happened while living there. Oh well, for now I am content with staying in the apartment, for I have not yet adjusted to the changes that have taken place while I was gone.

For example, automated machines now run many things, which, in my opinions is bad. This country has always had a problem with obesity, but now it's even worse because no one has to do anything that requires energy anymore. Just the other day the guys and I went to the store and there were no cash registers, just strange tunnel looking things towards the front of the store. Frank explained to me, somewhat annoyedly, that all you have to do is pass your cart through the tunnel and the thing rings up the items and bags them for you – better than any bagger too I've heard. I asked him, "What happens if you don't have a cart?" – "You *always*, have a cart," he answered indignantly.

Also, it seems that computers, like I explained before, have changed a lot. Now, many things are virtual, including the Internet. While online, you have swim goggle looking things on that allow you to see everybody (a character at least) and everything in 3D. There, you can move around and check your mail at a HUGE community mailbox. It all sounds fantastical, but I'm willing to give it a try.

There are a lot of other things, but I can't remember them right now, so I'm sure I'll write about it later, until then, good day!

9/2 3:31 p.m.

This week was busy.

It's colder outside today, about sixty-three degrees and it's only the beginning of September. Oh well, I'm used to the cold, my old concrete floor wasn't always the warmest thing in the world.

It's been almost a week since I've been released and I haven't had any *major* problems. I'm still having social fears and am finding it harder to adjust to the hectic non-routine life in which the guys are subjecting me to. It seems like there's never enough time in the day to do all of the things that I want or need to get done. Just the other day, I had to pick up some things from my old house, meet the guys for lunch, look up school information, and go to a job interview. So you see, things like this aren't always good for me, but fortunately, I handled it well enough for government standards.

Yesterday's interview went very well though and they called me the next day. So now, I have a job at 22-Hour Fitness as a personal trainer. Apparently, my qualifications were outstanding – three years of weight training and health and fitness classes. The job pays well (twenty-five fifty an hour), so I can now pay rent, pay for school, and can also afford some leisure activities, and on top of all that, I can get back into shape – ain't it great?

It's funny, the guys think I'm a bit more eccentric than I used to be, as in I steal the condiments and plasticware from fast food restaurants, talk to myself, and am able to keep myself occupied and have more fun with simple made-up games as opposed to the computer or TV. But, since I'm paying for part of the rent, they don't mind or mention any of what I do too much, and we all generally get along well, just like always – except when someone is grouchy.

Also, I got back in touch with a lot of my old, good friends, which of course makes me very happy. In fact, I am going to a Rave with one of them tomorrow; I'll write about that later.

So ah, I'm very satisfied with how my life is getting back on track so far, wait until I tell my family, they'll be so happy for me...I hope...Ah, I'm sure they will be, especially Uncle

Bill, he's cool like that, used to be a psychologist. Gee all I need now is a girlfriend...☺...Well, I have to get ready for work, I'll write later, ta ta...

9/6 4:25 p.m.

The Rave.

I love Techno. It was pretty fun, not much really to talk about; I mostly sat at the table listening to the music while watching everyone else dance. Brittany tried to get me to join her but I was way too nervous. Dancing is like trying to lick your back, it's difficult to do, and once you get it right, it looks funny anyway...or at least that's what my dancing is like. Besides, most everyone was on ecstasy anyway, and I really don't want to take part in the destruction of my brain. I have enough problems as it is without adding some mind-altering drug to it. Of course...I am taking another drug to mess with my mind...but that's not the point! The point is I don't trust pink octagonal shaped pills.

Of course, I had to drive home because Brittany and her friends were all either too high or too tired to drive. It was certainly a scary ride. I never got my license, but had my permit for almost a year, but that was a long time ago. I think I would have been fine though, except that Brittany likes to race her car, so it is a standard, not an automatic. Luckily though, the gear shifter is an up and down arrow on the steering wheel, but there is still a clutch, so that made it difficult. I don't think anyone in the car really noticed though, because like I said, they were all too high or too drunk and are used to bumpy rides.

Anyway, I eventually dropped off Brittany's friends and then took her to the apartment, laid her on the couch (she parties way too hard and I thought it'd be safer if I brought her here). I covered her up, and am now writing on the floor next to her, ready to go to sleep myself.

So that was my night, and it's early in the morning again. I think I have a big day tomorrow…or today…I don't remember. But, I'm off too bed, fun morning.

9/7 4:50 a.m.

I've missed a lot.

Wow, I'm out of the worldly loop as far as many things are concerned. Freedom of thought is dead. In fact, things are beginning to take on a more plastic look than I originally thought. Things are beginning to look like the book, A Brave New World. Everything is run by some kind of corporation or by the use of soma/ecstasy (not just in Raves!). I know it's not seriously as bad as the book, but it does look like no one is able to think for themselves anymore. When I walk around the streets – which isn't as often as I'd like – people seem apathetic towards everything, especially each other. Self-Absorption mixed with Propaganda plus Paranoia and You equals SAPPY, which is what this world has become. But then, I suppose things have been like this for a long time, just not as prevalent, or perhaps I just didn't notice. Either way, it bothers me because it seems that the corporations have taken over the people and our way of life more than the government has or has been able to, and because of that, things now seem to be better, but not in a good way. They've done this through the massive use of propaganda and by telling people what they NEED to have to survive. Thereby controlling the minds of the people and phasing out the parts of us (whether it is tools or thoughts) that makes us instinctual humans with a purpose. Now we are all becoming mindless drones buying the shiniest toy with the most buttons, which in reality accomplishes nothing more than whatever it is replacing. For example, VHS is dead, giving way to DVD, and the newly forming optical chips; which only gives you the ability to watch behind the scenes crap, a supposed better picture, and push more buttons. Personally, I'd rather watch a movie for the thought-provoking plot, not the behind the scenes BS and a clearer picture; it's surreal.

But then on the other side of the coin there are the people that *try* to think for themselves and only end up with one solution, and that is to screw up the system and their lives with some kind of horrible, crime ridden life-style. Out of all the life-style choices, you pick crime? What is the point of that, to beget the image of being a rebel? It's pointless, because you will always eventually get caught, and no one wants to get caught, because that'll change their image from a criminal, to a loser…I'm being a pessimist, I'm sure there are still people out there that don't buy into the aforementioned garbage, because they think like me, or because they just can't afford it, but even if they can't afford it, they will eventually rationalize into thinking like me, or they will put themselves into billions of dollars worth of debt.

Oh well, until we have thought police, I'll have nothing to worry about, and nor will anyone else. For until that happens, we all still have limited First Amendment Rights that insure our ability to do or say whatever we want, in moderation, so long as it does not impede or piss off any one group that can substitute its name with an acronym or ends with -ists. But then it's always been like this, only now the decline has escalated to a level far lower than any high I could ever reach no matter how low I squat, because, for every reform, people will always find a way to cheat the system and or ruin the ideals of others. It is a simple matter of Physics; for every action there is an equal and opposite reaction; it is an undeniable truth in our universe, and things will never change, save for the tools that we use to make those reactions and the peoples' names that carry out the actions, for people are also the same, and in a constant cycle of rebirth. It is sad but comforting that our world is nothing more than a gigantic blue and green rerun of itself, constantly supplying the same changes and entertainment for its unsuspecting audiences, where the only thing that truly changes is the individual mind and the things that are socially acceptable to the masses...So like I said, I'm out of touch, and am old school.

But on the plus side, root beer still exists, and Yoo-Hoo now makes many different flavors of milk like substance. But that's enough for today, I'm all out of things to notice and bitch about – TO ALL A GOOD NIGHT!

9/9 12:04 p.m.

National Day of Remembrance.

I forgot that today is an important day in the history of America. Nine years ago today, the "War on Terror" began, and to this day, it has not stopped.

I was in seventh grade at the time, I remember walking into class and my English teacher being absolutely stunned, and about to cry at what had happened. Of course, at the time, I did not know what had happened. I later made the connection between the report on the radio and the scenes on TV. That morning, every single class had their TV turned on to the news – some teacher's had to create paperclip antennas to see clearly – and we all watched in horror as both New York Trade Center buildings fell to the ground. I, sadly, was not so moved by the event because it seemed unreal to me that something like that, which seemed so far away and movie like, could actually happen. For, as a young teen, I had decided that both my country and I were invincible to things of this nature. I had unknowingly sheltered myself from the real world and from what was actually going on beyond my front door. I think that that was about the same time that I decided to further my naïveté and stopped watching TV. It was that moment where I decided to live in the moment and stopped caring…much like many others did. Hmm…I never really thought about it like that before…

Anyway, after that, many people found God, as they do in most crises. But hate crimes began again and as much fun as that sounds, it only got worse. Luckily though, at the time we had a very Christian and very compassionate president, George Bush. He was not much of a public speaker, often times stumbling over his own words and pausing when his vice president would take a drink of water – very shady. Despite this though, I respected him more than the ones before and the ones after him because of his ability to tell the truth, cry on TV, and take control of the country in a time of need. Granted he did not always have a good reason for doing things, or did not have a reason period, he was still better, and for his short four-year term, brought this sad-shaped country together.

Now though, it is a day of remembrance for *all* of the people, buildings, and cities that have been destroyed in order to eliminate terrorism. We have so far succeeded in lowering the number of terrorists, but have only made the remaining terrorists angry and have given them more reasons to fight for what they think is right. The war wages on, but has become something less spectacular, and is no longer considered a big deal, but is something that has been pushed to the background as an everyday occurrence.

Anyway, I just thought I'd mention the important day of the year because it's an important day of the year. But I'm off. Good day.

9/11 10:45 a.m.

Something that I've noticed.

Any outside observer would find that the guys and I are all three almost complete opposites. Somehow though, that is exactly why we are all the best of friends. It seems to me that if we were all alike, we would become subjects of a terribly gory horror movie.

Isaac for example, being my best friend since first grade, is for one, shorter than Frank and me, has long dark maroon colored hair (he dyes it so I have no idea what color it really is anymore), and is unkempt. He is the most introverted of the three of us, but at the same time is the most out-going, because he'll quietly do anything you can think of. He was brought up in a family whose moralistic views were based on that of the hippie days, only with a nineties type of reformation. Because of that, Isaac has grown up able to accept almost anything and everything, and will also do anything and everything within reason (we both hate drugs and things of this nature). With that, he has developed a very keen sense of humor, and around us two, you would never know he is the quiet one. His history is also very interesting.

While in middle school, he developed an obsession with a certain someone that led to two years of clinical depression. He never saw a counselor, so Frank and I took it upon ourselves to help him through it. We seemed to help a little bit, but he finally came to terms with his obsession on his own, when his first girlfriend replaced the obsession. Suddenly, his mood took a Mount McKinley peak for the better. Since then he hasn't dropped down again, except for during major events, as all of us do. Strangely though, Frank and I were never able to completely understand the reason for his depression because even Isaac didn't know the real reasons. Now, no one really cares because it's all over and we're still all alive. Anyway though, Isaac is a good kid, he's a little too carefree sometimes, but he's smart, knows how to live life, and has lots of different types of friends all over the place because of how he is. We met in first grade (the "First Year of Hell" I call it), and on through the remaining years of hell we had classes together every once in a while, and became friends that way. It especially helped that he ironically lived in the neighborhood across from mine. We never really kept in touch over the phone, but that's mostly because we saw each other nearly every day in school throughout our entire school career. In high school especially, we would spend lunch together, walking to various restaurants and spending the lot of our time at the Quiggly's. Unfortunately, we stopped spending lunchtime and other time together when his girlfriend came into the picture. We stopped talking as much and hanging-out because he felt it necessary to spend every waking moment with her. But it's all good; whenever we talk, there is a history behind it, so thick that everything is like an inside joke – hardly anyone ever understands us. I like it.

Frank on the other hand, is a "Big Tall Korean Man" as I call him, because he's six foot two inches tall, weighing in at one hundred ninety-two pounds, three time WWF Champion, with an IQ of 130,…just kidding. But seriously, he *is* a big tall Korean man with an IQ of 130. He and I are closer in personality than Isaac and I, but that's because we both grew up in a similar type of household. His dad was much like my mom in the fact that he would freak out at all kinds of small things. But at the same time, I had a lot more freedom, whereas Frank's dad was Chinese, and would hardly let him do ANTYHING outside of the house. So, he grew up being a computer kid, and so did I, only he was obsessed with it (wanted to bring it on our camping trip), when I could live without it for a while, and enjoyed getting out of the house more often than not. Then, if his dad wasn't enough, his mom was complete opposite, and would let him do whatever he wanted, and in fact was about the nicest little lady I've ever met. These two parents put together, turned Frank into a very independent, intelligent, hyper, semi-extroverted, well-mannered, big tall Korean man. Of course, for the fact that he still has a hold on reality and isn't as street-smart, he finds me weird, and the majority of the time we are jokingly pointing this out to each other (usually loudly in public), heh, in fact, I think that's how we met. We were in sixth grade band class together, and we started our friendship by rudely criticizing the other's music playing since we both have a large ego. After several months of this, we somehow became friends (of course, I thought he was annoying and was suspicious for the same reason I'm annoyed and suspicious about everyone else). After that, we were inseparable, especially since he called me every damned night! We ended up in the same band class every year until high school, but kept in touch during that mess as well. It's funny; we talked so much in band, that both of us started playing very horribly (have to remember I was first chair in sixth grade, the beginning of seventh, and only once in eighth), in fact we even made "SHUT UP!" cards that we'd flash at each other whenever the other person was talking (this was so we wouldn't fail, and also so we could go to Disneyland). Wow, the stories I could tell about band...maybe another time. Anyway, so we kept in touch, and our best friend relationship took place over the phone, several hours a day usually, and has continued on since then.

Then there's me, taller than Isaac but shorter than Frank, only somewhat in touch with reality, brought up stricter than Isaac and not as strict as Frank. So I guess I'm the cream that holds the cookie together so-to-speak, because no group is complete without it's semi-buff, genius sociopath with a tendency to hurt people for being stupid and the ability to save someone from themselves by listening and by making odd, thought provoking comments at odd times throughout a conversation. ☺

Both of them mean the world to me though, and I love them dearly in a strictly platonic sense. So, I hope that we all keep in touch and or live together and or live close by to each other forever. I know it's possible because I've read stories about it, and even my dad would visit his best friend since first grade all the time, and I'm just like my dad, so I will too!

But anyway, I have to go do some chores, and finish some enrollment paperwork for school. Good day!

9/15 1:11 p.m.

Hanging-out.

For the fact that I will be going back to school again soon, and because the guys and I all have jobs, we've decided that we should go out whenever possible. Usually we go to the movies – there are some good ones still coming out after all – the arcade (they love this weird dancing game, and I love the virtual reality cop games), go carts, or just to other peoples' houses. These things are what we all have in common no matter what, for, fun is a universal language, and at the same time, is teaching me how to come back to what I used to be like – fun and excitable – instead of the semi-deadpan personality that I've developed over the past few years.

Anyway, today we went over to Rikki's house, one of Isaac's friends, and watched people snort crack lines. None of us knew this would be going on, so we stayed for a while, but in the interest of not getting involved, we left. While I was there, I learned one thing: Drugs are bad. It truly is disgusting to watch people destroy themselves like that, I mean, of all the things you can do now-a-days to get your mind off of things, they still choose primitive drugs, and snorting!? I guess I was just brought up as a D.A.R.E kid that's all, that and if you visit downtown of any city, you'll see exactly what drugs do to people. It sends them to the streets, on a constant search for another, better high. The idea of addiction doesn't bother me because that's what happens when you like something, but the thing someone has become addicted to, is what the problem is.

Dancing for example, is healthy, it releases tension and is just fun/funny to do and watch. Drugs on the other hand, screw with your brain – I like mine the way it is thank you very much – kills relationships, your life, and you. It's stupid, pointless, and near impossible to get out of, so I choose not to take part in it, and luckily neither do any of my friends.

Instead, we drove around town looking for something to do, checking out the new parts of town, and seeing if there were any arcades, restaurants, or race tracks we hadn't been to yet. We didn't expect to find anything, for we always seem to be driving around looking for something to do. But! Much to our surprise, we found the Pancake Stop; one of the last ones left in the country after they were all shut down for some forgettable reason. This one though, was family owned, and therefore exempt from any company mishaps, and in fact was much better in service and in quality than any company Pancake House I have EVER been to. So, at three something p.m., we all had pancakes in front of us that could smile while being eaten. They were good n' tasty. ☺ But that's when the cool part happened. While I was eating the eyes off of my pancakes, about eight Elvis's, each varying in size, figure, and hair shape, all walked in wearing homemade Elvis jumpsuits. To say the least, I about pissed myself at the frightening sight, and so did everyone else in the restaurant. After the shock wore off though, I continued to devour my happy pancake man, and noticed that the guys were still staring. I told them that if they were so interested, they should go get their autographs. And, after some coaxing and a lot of poking and annoying whines, all three of us convinced each other to go at once, to get all eight Elvis's autographs. It went a little something like this:

(All of us giggling like schoolboys and talking in purposely-nerdy voices) "Can we have your autographs!" – "Well sure kids!" (Surprisingly good accents too) – "Gee whiz that sure is nice of you sirs!" – "Thank you, thank you very much" (they all said in creepy unison).

Ok, after closer inspection you'd kind of have to be there, but at least now I have a big Pancake House napkin with eight different signatures, all reading "Elvis Presley"! It's exciting I know! Ok, I'm done. But at least my day was fun! Anyway, after that we just sat in our booth wondering what to do next. After about half an hour of sitting and thinking and talking about what to do next, we decided it was time to leave. So we drove to the charging station to recharge the car and got some soda, the best kind, Blue Freeze, which now has enough caffeine in each bottle to kill a small horse and or cure someone's headaches for two years pending. There we sat for about another five minutes, until we were being honked at; we decided to go to the community college, so that I could check out the campus.

The campus is of decent size, three stories, fifty acres with a playing field, a practice field, and several separate buildings that house the library, administrations office, and some vocational buildings, all very small comparatively. The plastic, flame-proof material – which isn't really flame-proof, but will melt, not burn – was painted a dark shade of gray, with each section (art, music, literature, etc.) painted different, sickly colors so that the students could find their classes easier. Despite the nauseating paint job though, I felt that I would have an odd sense of pride for my soon-to-be place of learning.

By the time we had finished everything, it was about time for me to go to work, and about time for the other two to sit on the computer and or TV until the butt crack of dawn. There they will stay until sleep over takes them or they have go to work themselves. So we headed home, picked up my work clothes, and Frank gave me a ride to work, where I slaved feverishly over work-out machines, work-out plans, and people working-out, and just about anything else that was work-out related...I love my job, it's so easy. ☺

But it's really early in the morning now, so I must be off to sleep or play video games, or read, or one of the many things that stimulates the brain in one fashion or another...good morning.

9/21 6:08 a.m.

My first month in short.

It's been about a month now since I've been released, and needless to say everything has been A-OK. Despite my original stress about social situations and getting school started up again, which I seem to have not written about strangely enough, I have not really had anything but good times.

Before I left the hospital, I thought that I would either end up right back, or that wherever I happened to land, would be my own Mental Ward, walls filled with inane babble, and me rocking in the corner of a room, waiting for some sort of relief. Instead though, I live with my two best friends, have a job, am forming new acquaintances – not as many as I'd like though, yet – and am getting my life somewhat back on track. I find it very interesting and suppose that perhaps someone that is big, has a three-letter name, and has lived forever, might be smiling upon me...or if I want to be an ass I can just blame my pharmaceuticals. Either way, it works well and I thank them both.

It looks like I've neglected my journal lately, and haven't written down all that's been going on. In fact, I think I've only written a few entries, and wish that I had written more about my growth as a person. Oh well though, the growth has been so small that it's actually quite hard to put into words...maybe during school something will happen and I can write about it. Maybe I'll find divine truth or enlightenment, or something *like* that – Ha! Or perhaps I'll just learn something and get a girlfriend, either way it works well for me. ☺ As far as my writing though, I'll try to do it more often. Then again maybe it's good that I'm not writing as much, because I am keeping myself busy, and also it tells me that there isn't as much inner conflict anymore…Hmm, oh well, I must go as usual because there are babies to kiss and autographs to sign…good day!

9/30 11:01 a.m.

6
Reality Sets in

Today was "normal."

Rrr! I haven't written in so long that I'm actually mad at myself for it! It's finally time for school to start and I'm just about ready to begin. I've got all of my materials, the last of my paperwork is done, and oh my God there is a lot. I've decided that neither corporations nor the government rule the world, but PAPERWORK does! Ok not really, but it sure as hell seems like it! I've got my class schedule finally. I will be taking calculus second semester, English III second semester, and government second semester to make up for the mandatory classes I missed in high school. My electives are musical composition and computer graphics – have to leave my options open. Also, since I was in band from fifth to ninth grade while playing the French horn and piano on the side, I figured musical composition was the next logical step. Also, I've always liked music of all kinds, so I figured composing it wouldn't be that bad of an idea, especially since I used to write a lot of my own stuff and or add things during practice. I also happen to think computer generated graphics are awesome, so

I would like to learn how to do that incase I get bored one day and want to impress someone.

I'm hoping that I can keep my grades up when school starts because 22-Hour Fitness gives bonuses to people going through school with a 3.0 GPA or higher. I've been saving up money for a car, that way I don't have to take the crappy old green city buses anymore, and or bum rides off of people. So far, I have almost three thousand dollars saved up from this year, it's easy to save when you live with friends and don't have too much rent money to pay, plus I had other accumulated money in my savings from years before. I've always thought that the old DeLorean was cool, ever since I saw it on "Back to the Future," but it's fifty-three thousand dollars, so I figure I'll go for something a bit cheaper. Especially since most of my money will be for insurance. Luckily though, I live in a medium sized city, so insurance and car prices aren't so high. Plus whatever I get will probably still be run by gas, and right now gas prices are at an all time high, two dollars and eighty-eight cents a gallon, whereas electric prices are only about fifty cents a megawatt.

Other than that though, I've been busy trying to revive my social life. It is slowly coming back to the way it used to be, when everywhere I went I knew someone to a greater or lesser extent. Though, I keep running into the same problems as always because I'm too suspicious of people and generalize them into the "stupid box" too quickly. No matter, I'm getting better, I promise!

Oh yah, speaking of girls, I almost had a girlfriend for a while there. She was a pretty cool kid, very sexy too, but she freaked out and stopped talking to me when she found out that I wasn't lying about being in a mental hospital…makes me wonder how she found out it was true. I guess that not everyone can appreciate mental health. I'll just have to find a girl that likes my eccentricities I guess. Oh well, who needs girls, they just drag you down…Ah right, who am I kidding I need girls! ☺

Anyway, I need to write more, I'm sure I will when school starts getting interesting, good or bad, but nonetheless interesting. Good Day!

10/28 1:32 p.m.

Today was an Emergency!

I had a major emergency today! I RAN OUT OF ROOT BEER! That, is *definitely* something that I want never to happen again! I mean, besides the fact that I'm totally obsessed with root beer has absolutely *nothing* to do with it! ☺ Then again, I love milk too, and I have a lot of that, so I think I'll drink some with my cereal instead of root beer this time.

Other than the root beer incident though, everything's been going great, it seems that the only problems that I've had, are root beer related. I'm doing well in all of my classes for once – motivation is key – and I wrote my first song with music to it today! I took the guys with me to one of those goofy little coffeehouses that I was told about, and played my song there. Everyone seemed to like it; I received many finger snaps for it. I swear those places are funny in the scariest way possible, with all the weird little people and their big huge coffee cups with oversized foam on them. Not to mention the horrible COLD COFFEE! What the *hell* is the point of that!? Coffee is supposed to be a caffeine filled hot drink that makes you constipated, not a cold drink that makes you nauseated. The heat is there to help wake you up, not make you puke! Hell, I've seen people drink cold coffee in the dead of winter; it's stupid, I have no idea where they think of these things. Besides, I'd prefer Hot Chocolate any day. Nevermind, this is a moot point.

I've noticed recently that my self-esteem has been pretty high, I better be careful, if someone notices, they might take it upon themselves to ruin it. I'm still somewhat dependent on what others say or think of me...depending on who it is anyway. If it's some peon that I don't know, I don't think I'd care too much because obviously they don't know me very well at all. However, if it were a friend or someone I know, it would seriously damage me in one way or another, unless of course the person was obviously joking, but even then I would have some issues. It's difficult sometimes to tell if someone is joking though, especially if they make an off color comment on the square. Freudian Slip I say. Crazy people out there, glad I'm not one ☺.

I'm listening to Weird Al Yankovic; he's the BEST EVER! I have all sixteen of his CDs, it's a shame he died, he was an awesome guy, I really think he was a genius. I mean, anyone can write a song or a poem and add music to it, but it takes a *real* genius to turn the original lyrics into something funny that make sense, and also matches all of the syllables, rhythms, and other such parts of the original song. I think I'm going to continue his legacy when I finish my music composition class and make my own parodies. Or not, who knows, I probably will have bigger, better things to do by then, but it's still a good idea.

I have a crush on someone; I met her in my government class. I became interested in her on the first day when the professor asked if anyone understood what our government's role in society was. She answered the question almost exactly as I would: with a tone of dignity, slight hints of sarcasm in her more optimistic statements, and slight pride only when her answer seemed to be affirmed. It's taken me the whole first week, but I started talking to her, got her number, and we've talked on the phone ever since. We then decided that we both have a lot in common and that it would be interesting to start dating. For now, I won't be telling her anything of my past, and if she asks, I'll probably side step the question. It's not honest I know, but I don't want to scare this one away. Otherwise, nothing big has happened, but I'm sure there will be something more about her that I can write later.

It's late though, and I'm hungry, so I think that I'll go eat some cereal at...one o'clock in the morning...that works...of course it does, my step-dad used to make breakfast at nine p.m. all the time so who cares. Good morning.

11/6

This class is boring.

I'm sitting in class right now and nothing interesting is happening. In fact, I'm just about to fall asleep again, I hate calculus, it's such a horribly useless bit of math. When the hell am I ever going to use it unless I decide to become a NASA engineer? Oh well, who cares, I guess that's why I've been bringing my journal with me, so I can write about class while I'm in class, "A smart one he is" they'd say.

Right now, I have a B in this class, so all I really have to do is my homework and I'm set, well, if I do my homework correctly anyway. It's not that hard though, I guess I just understand math, I was especially good at algebra. That's strange because I normally work better with things if I can picture them in my mind and work them out like in Geometry. Algebra, though, is just a bunch of variables that you pull out of thin air, as opposed to Geometry's solid shapes and all that wonderful spatial stuff. Actually, come to think of it I don't even really like math; I prefer science. If it weren't for the fact that science is filled with annoying memorization and millions of years of school, I'd major in that. I'm lazy though, so I'm taking the easy road – music – maybe if I go to college I'll pursue something that's science related or maybe it'll just be a life-hobby. Either way, learning is fun and I don't care if that

119

sounds corny or not because it's true. In fact, I'd love school if it wasn't so mentally, emotionally, physically, and socially demanding – I don't take well to stress. It's strange that I haven't had any problems yet.

Usually, I get really intense about school and start losing a lot of energy, which leads to grouchiness, which then leads to more stress, which then eventually leads to some sort of breakdown, and that's never good. In fact, I think that might have been what caused my original problems. Of course, for the fact that school has only been on for about two or three weeks, is why none of the aforementioned have happened yet. Unless of course, I'm seriously cured and there won't be any problems at all, but I guess I'll just have to see because I doubt one hundred percent recovery can happen this fast.

Oh look, he's saying something important, I should listen, I'll write again in my next class or sometime later today or tomorrow or this week or this month or just whenever I happen to need to etc. etc.! Ok I'm done, good day.

11/8 Period 1

English classes are exciting!

NOT! Oh my God I hate English so much. I speak English – my mom always used to yell at me for getting bad grades in my "mother tongue," made me want to hit her – and as far as I'm concerned I write quite well. I mean, what is literature but the handwritten or typed words of a person's mind. As long as the person doing the writing is happy with what they see, it should not matter how "structured" etc. it is. Of course, I suppose I see the need for the class, because when it comes to sharing these writings with people, some may be happy with their own BS and incoherent, irrational mumbling on paper, whereas, when it comes to real life, the ideal of writing beautifully, properly, and for a reason is very much more important. In fact, it is sometimes the difference between twenty thousand and one hundred thousand dollars a year. So, in the interest of increasing my future salary, I will sit through the class, but I will be despondent and stubborn throughout the year. Unless of course Professor Ganges proves to be a good person, so far he is a bit eccentric, but then so am I, perhaps we'll get along.

Maybe though, I'm not giving the class a chance; I haven't had very good experiences with English classes in the past. My sixth grade teacher was always very nice to everyone, including me, so it was hard to tell if my writing was ever good, or if she was just glad that I tried. In seventh grade, my teacher was an ex-high school teacher, and a hippie to boot. His room was filled the type of things you would find in a seventies novelty shop; Fish Head Music posters, Beetles memorabilia, toys of all sorts, and a gigantic collection of CDs and other such music related items, most of which were inappropriate for us to listen to. In the sternest way possible though, he taught my Honors class how to diagram a sentence, how to write an expository essay, and how to write good stories. He did this by having us all copy, word for word, the definition of every type of word known to the English language (I never copied word for word, probably why I failed his class, but learned despite and to spite it). Also, we were required to turn in a story of any kind, every Monday, write journals about anything everyday, and finish two major projects, one per semester.

In the first semester, I was teamed up with Frank and the goody-two-shoes of the class. We were to draw-up an entire election campaign for the current running governors at the time (our goody-two-shoes played that governor, fittingly of course). After several painstaking months the project was finished, and my group failed only semi-miserably, however, I was not so lucky. For the fact that my grade in that class had fallen below a C, I was moved down to "developmental"

English, the worst thing to happen to an apathetic, grouchy, stressed-out, and hateful seventh grader. Just as my luck would have it, things got worse from there, for the first time in years it snowed profusely and I was stranded back east with my Dad for an extra week after Winter Break. My grade in developmental dropped to an F. For the rest of the year I tried haphazardly to bring my grade up, and the only thing that saved me, was the pre-formatted, rigorous research essay on a now obsolete fighter jet, the F-14 Tomcat. I passed that class with flying colors – a D – and moved on to "Regular" English the next year.

Luckily though, eighth grade was when things began looking up again. My social life hit a turn with the sudden booming meeting and growth of a relationship with Jane. Also, my eighth grade English teacher interested me in my first real novel, <u>1984</u>, and I haven't stopped reading since. Also, she was not at all obsessed with teaching us how to write formatted essays. In fact, her main concern was to teach us how to like books and the things that surround them. Her main source of information from and for the students was through debate and class discussion – there were twelve people in my class. My favorite way of learning is by listening and thinking things over out loud with someone. Therefore, I was in love with her class.

After middle school, ninth and tenth grade English were exact replicas of seventh and eighth grade; Honors, then regular, which moved up to Honors because the teacher was convinced that I could write as well, if not better, than her AP seniors. It was neither exciting nor was there new information, ever. I learned nothing, and passed the classes like they were frozen green lights in empty traffic.

Eleventh grade though, was different, for my teacher was like that of my seventh grade teacher, but in a much different way. She was more interested in teaching diction, full structure, and so much more, that I learned how to write poetically and correctly. In fact, after her class I had several of my own poems published and won several awards – which I never collected for the fact that I did not want to spend two thousand dollars just to get a "possible winner" medal.

Now I am in a class one step higher, and a finale of, my eleventh grade class.

Crap! I have to go, teacher's asking me questions, I'll write later or next period! BYE!

I went out with a girl today.

Joyce came over today so I gave her the tour of the apartment. She seemed amazed that an apartment lived in by three guys was so clean and I assured her that Cleanliness is next to Godliness. She didn't believe me, so I told her the truth; we hire people off of the street to clean it every once in a while and whatever ends up in their pockets by the end of the day is theirs to keep and that's why there's not very much crap lying around. Again she didn't believe me so I pretended to cry and moved on to another subject. For a while she continued to be amazed at the seemingly woman's touch in our man apartment until she saw what was in the kitchen. Nothing. We have milk, bread, peanut butter, honey, eggs, a lot of sugar packets, and other related fast-food condiments. After five minutes of staring into the pantry, hoping for something new to suddenly appear, we decided to go out.

We started walking in the general direction of somewhere, at the time we did not know where we were going, but continued to walk anyway. After about a mile of ideas and another mile of deciding we ended up at Lampard's Home of Throwed Rolls. Such an awesome place, family owned. Surprisingly, the line wasn't very long today and we were seated within the hour.

Lampard's is one of the best restaurants I've ever been to. Not only do they throw fresh made rolls at you from across the room, but they also pass around odd side dishes, and to top it all off, EVERYTHING is all you can eat – reasonably priced too. We ordered the basket of chicken together because we're both cheap, like chicken (I like dark she likes white), and can have as much as we want, very economical. I think together we ended up finishing three baskets worth, including half a dozen rolls and several ladles full of side dishes – we were full.

We walked back to the apartment and watched TV while the chicken settled and made itself comfortable in our stomachs. There was nothing on, so we played connect four instead. She beat me. I never was good at connect four and I now hate it! Just kidding, it's fun, but ah. Then Frank got home from work and made several strange, nonsensical comments about me having a girl at the house alone. I told him to sit on it n' twist, then continued playing with Joyce. We continued playing for a while but soon noticed that it was late, so I walked her to her car – why didn't we drive to the restaurant...oh well – and said those fateful words, "Today was fun, we should do it again sometime." She smiled broadly and inside I jumped around in circles while she said, "Yes it was. Call me." YAY! I'm officially "dating." I'll call her later, right now I have to go hit Frank. Until then, good day!

11/10 11:10 p.m.

Today was interesting.

As I've said before I enjoy music. So, I went to a concert.

One of my "neighbors" in music class invited me to a Trekkers concert with him and his group of friends. I was flattered to say the least and accepted graciously, but needed a ride. Luckily though, they were all planning to take a large, "Class two Hippie Van," as I sometimes call them. In the interest of making transit easier for all, I went over to his – Sean's – house. It was about the messiest place I had ever been in, or at least of late, but at the same time seemed cozy and rather livable. Of course, its livability would only last for a day or so because after that I would probably start to clean it myself, but none of that has anything to do with anything, so I'll leave it alone. Anyway, we played on his computer for a while; computer technology is extraordinary nowadays, as far as graphics are concerned, not to mention the amount of space and type of systems, but I think I've already mentioned this once before, so I'll skip the Ooing and Ahing for now. We hung-out until it was time to go, mostly playing Virtual Tsunami Tank Wars, watching movies, and making food. Sean's a pretty cool kid as far as I'm concerned, older than I am too, seems to know how to live life to the fullest and in the cheapest way possible – best combination.

We collected the others – Little Joe, Heather, José, Brittany, and AJ – and headed for the Sound Stage, a pint-sized version of the school's theater room. In fact, the place was so small that if I had jumped, my head would have gone through the ceiling. The concert started half an hour late, which was fine because it gave us all a chance to get acquainted. Turns out the name Little Joe has nothing to do with his height and in fact, has an interesting story behind it. However, I don't think I'll write it here...

Unfortunately, Trekkers is a hardcore punk band, which means that they specialize in discouraging, misguided, loudly annoying lyrics about society, the government, and how often they masturbate. Some of their songs were exciting, but for the most part were just stupid and full of swearing. It's sad really, in the eighties, punk rock was a bloom of intelligent drop-outs singing real songs about what was seriously wrong with life at the time. The second or third verse of the eighties punk bands would always propose some kind of solution to the problem being recognized in the song, unlike the Trekkers constant reiteration of the same thing in different words and or solos. Sadly though, now, punk is dying, and is being revived by the angst dropouts with inhibitions, drinking problems, and drug habits – which is similar to eighties punkers, only without goals or fresh ideas. Then, when they run out of dick and fart joke songs, they begin ruining classic songs by singing them loudly and with their version of music; it sounds horrible. Oh well, to each their own. I seem have a lot to say about nothing don't I? Hell, with all the bitching I do, I could probably become a punk rock star myself!

Besides, the night actually wasn't bad, at least I got out of the house, met new people, and got to watch drunks at a concert – that's always exciting. I personally don't enjoy getting drunk unless it's for a special occasion: wedding, funeral, birthday, graduation, and things of this nature. I once had the idea of working at a bar, just for personal entertainment, but decided against it because the majority of drunk people actually start more bar fights, are jerks, and are ugly, then are ones who are funny to watch.

Afterwards we all went out to Jerry's, apparently many people go there after a concert because it's quiet, good for calming down after loud music and massive use of ecstasy. So we sat around there for about two hours building houses out of straws, silverware, creamers, and whatever else they inadvertently provided us with. I mostly listened to them talk, and by the sound of it, they have a lot of history together. I found out that they're all a year or two older than I am, which makes me feel cooler because I'm with the big kids. They seem to enjoy taking part in many strange activities, most of which are illegal, but not important enough for anyone to care. One of the more interesting/queer parts of them, is their obsession with making "meat puppets." At first I thought they were trying to suggest something obscene and only slightly disgusting, but when we ended up at Shop n' Save buying ground beef and other related food products, then headed to Little Joe's house, I found out that they were seriously, Meat...Puppets. In the interest of being a good sport, I took part in the making of one of these puppets, mine resembling the president about as much as meat possibly can. However, the horrendous smell of cooking multi-meat was more than unappetizing, so I let them eat mine.

After that though, they passed around several drinks with varying percentages of alcohol in them, so I asked to be taken home before everyone was too drunk to drive. Sean took me home in the "Moving Van," as he calls it, and when I got home Isaac and Frank were up waiting for me much like TV parents do – probably because we're all insomniacs, but I like to think they care. Right away, they asked me where I was, for, I had forgotten to inform them of my every move today. They were "disappointed" in me, and said that I shouldn't be home later than one A.M., but said that they'd let it go this time. They're so nice, I sure wish my parents were like them. Funny. So now, I'm going to have to find a way to be home later than one every day. Just kidding, today was probably the extent of my outside life, for, as much as I enjoyed being with Sean and his friends, I'm not so much into punk rock concerts, making meat-puppets, and getting drunk. I'll keep that to myself though, and just make some sort of excuse next time he invites me to a Trekkers concert or a band of the like mentality.

Strangely, I wasn't tired after all of that, so I stayed up with the guys to watch TV, I feel dirty now, but that's ok, there was nothing but infomercials and reruns of Friends on. We stayed entertained while making fun of the irrational propaganda used to sell products, "only fourteen payments of $19.99!" Yeah right, that's BS! For a metal spork!? No way I'll pay $2,800!

Anyway, it's four o'clock in the morning now, so I believe it's time for me to retire to my bed. Good dark morning.

11/13

Groups are funny people.

Lately I've been noticing, more and more, the differences between high school and community college people. There are some, but not as many as I originally thought. Perhaps that is because community college kids, sadly to say, are the less mature versions of college students. Of course, I've not been to college before, so maybe it's like this everywhere. Hopefully, when I'm released into the *real* world, for school is neither real nor public, things will be different.

What I'm talking about of course, are social classes, labels, standards, and stereotypes. In high school, you've got the Punkers, Skaters, Preps, Jocks, Nerds, Norms, Freaks, etc. Everyone sticks to his or her own group and only the few strong and courageous try to intermix and even fewer actually accomplish the intermixing. I personally, try to be one of those people, and have been learning to be more extroverted, however, am not sure if I'm successfully in "fitting-in" to multiple groups, but it's still fun to try. Now, this by itself is a fine system as far as letting people fit into where ever they can, this way there is no "in crowd," because the "in crowd" is whatever you happen to fit into as yourself. Of course, there's always the people that are one thing and want to be the other because they see one particular group as a higher class than them, when in reality, or at least in mine, we are all generally equal until proven otherwise – which I will explain later. I suppose I just thought that in a higher institution for learning, there would be a lot more intermixing between people, but in fact there is not, and it more closely resembles that of high school, only with taller, hairier people. Oh well, it does however, seem that everyone respects each other more often than not. What I used to see was each group complaining about the other group and then eventually plotting on them in an obvious manner; makes you wonder how things like Columbine and Brockington ever happened without anyone knowing beforehand. Luckily though, only the more immature groups – which are not restricted to any one label – still loudly proclaim their disgust for the others now. However, I still find it funny that these groups exist and that instead of disrespecting each other, they pretend that the other group does not exist at all, therefore, eliminating prejudices but also preventing understanding. Which is probably what my point of this entire paragraph was, but by now I really don't remember, so I'll move on to my next subject.

As far as respect is concerned, I believe that first impressions are the most important. I know I personally hate being judged from first impressions because there are times when I'm in a pissed off mood, a stupid mood, or just no mood at all, and don't want people thinking that I am like that all of the time. But I am a hypocrite most of the time, so that makes it okay for me to judge people from the way they walk, talk, act, sound, and or dress. However, the difference is, I usually keep these judgements to myself. Also, these judgements are always subject to change, in fact, I often go out of my way to test people so that those judgements *will* change.

I've noticed that I unconsciously give everyone two chances, depending on the circumstances and the person. If they screw up once in any way at all, I will usually see past it, but if they do it again or do something else, I seriously begin to reconsider that person's worth to me and how much I want to continue to speak with them etc.

I have no tolerance for people that blatantly disrespect my friends, good people, property of others, or me. In fact, I've been known to hurt a few people for disrespecting me, especially when he insulted my intelligence. I am not conceited, but I will not put up with someone, whom is obviously wrong and insistent upon it, especially when I know I'm right for whatever researched reason. In fact, stupidity is one of my pet peeves, for, of all the little annoyances in the world, someone's incompetence and inability to at least THINK about something really pisses me off. I understand if the person does not have the capacity to figure something out or has at least tried numerous times and still cannot understand something, but if you just sit there and don't even try to figure it out, then ask questions that have been answered SEVERAL times before, I'm going to have to freak-out and make a scene! I mean come on people, use your God given brain, it's there for a reason, stop thinking about meaningless garbage and LEARN something for once! I've seen so many people-parrots that when asked to explain things in their own words, have no idea how to and in fact, don't understand diddly-shit to begin with. I've seen it millions of times, it just makes me want to shoot that person because they have no business consuming and taking up space on this planet if they can't even grasp the simple concept of thinking for themselves! I don't even know how teachers can put up with some of the things kids think of, "you want an eight-hundred word essay? So like, how many pages is that?" – "It's eight-hundred words...how many ever pages it comes out to." – "But like...what if it's only two pages?" – "As long as it is eight-hundred words that's fine." – "Umm, I don't get it." That actually happened a few days ago too. Why can't people understand simple concepts like eight-hundred words is however many pages it fits on!? Of course, I listen, so I have no place to speak do I. Oh well, damned sheep.

Now that I'm mad, I think now is a good time to go get something to drink...don't know why, just sounds like a good idea. So I'm off, mad day.

11/16 1:50 p.m.

Paranormal happenings.

They call it, telepathy. I strange occurrence where two or more people can communicate with each other without speaking. It is rare in our society, for the majority of people have been overcome by simple tasks and alternate ways of communicating; such as Internet and phone. However, there are some people in this world that have decided to focus their inherent mental abilities and can now use their minds to communicate with one another, read minds, tell the future, move objects, and yes, even set fire to normally uninflammable objects (Details in Stephen King novels).

In this seemingly quaint town, in an apartment on Michael Way, live three young men whom have the startling ability to communicate telepathically. They call it, the "Mind-Link."

"This is on TV? COOL! Oh, the mind-link? Ah, it's really cool cause like we can sit there and not say anything and we all know what the other is thinking," says one of the inhabitants of apartment 2D.

"We've always had it, ever since seventh grade and it's always been growing. When my friend here got stuck in a mental hospital, yep that's right, he's a nut!"

"SHUT UP!"

"Sorry, he's, 'legally insane'"

"Thank you, continue."

"Anyway, while he was gone, Isaac and I lost it for a while. You see, it takes three people for it to work, it's like a triangle of…mind-powers, or something like that. Ah, well without him it started getting really loud in here so we went to go see him, hoping he would come back and much to our surprise he did."

"Ah, I guess in a strange sort of way I'm the glue that holds this whole thing together. Without me, they would have no one to make fun of or mess around with, and worst of all there would be no mind-link! Oh, what exactly is it? Well, when you've known these two morons for so long, you kind of get to know how and what they think and when they think it. It's sickening to be inside their heads but I'm sure mine is no prize either. Examples? Umm, umm…ok like…no…umm, hold on pause the thing while I think, I don't want to look like a dumbass on TV. Oh ah editors. I didn't know your show was still on. I should watch it. Oh nevermind we only get two thousand channels, we went for the lower costing cable. Anyway…umm…hold on, shut up…Ok like when we were watching this movie and the main character died, I screamed inside my head because I liked the guy, and they both turned to me and asked what I said. Obviously, I didn't say anything but they heard my mind-scream. Or one of us will be hungry and then the other one will get up and say let's go, we'll wonder where, and he'll say, 'to get something to eat, if you're going to keep bitching about being hungry then let's just go.' And No One said ANYTHING! It's amazing. That kind of thing happens a lot, we hear each other's thoughts…either that or we just think loudly…or both."

"No we've never thought about being a side-show thank you very much."

"Does it make good money?"

"SHUT UP!"

"Any more questions? No, we can't move things with our minds. No I can't read your mind."

"I CAN! You are thinking…'wow, these guys are a bunch of morons and I hate my job and I'm hungry and want coffee.' Here I made you some coffee and we have donuts if you want one."

"That's uncanny."

"Yes it is. I was right!? HA! That's awesome, well do you believe me now? No? Well I know that you're divorced but you still love her, you're ninety-seven, have had penile dysfunction, never went through college, your voice is a voice box, you enjoy water polo, you think your camera man is hot, and you enjoy chains, whips, and other bondage related things. Leaving so soon? Oh well. Bye Mr. Unsolved Mysteries man!"

"HAHA! You scared him away!"

"Dude how'd you know all of that?"

"I found it online."

"Heh."

"That's hilarious!"

"Yep whelp, what can I say?"

Well that was fun! Good day!

11/18 7:35 p.m.

I'm hyper!

Look! I made a song!

Lalala, I like food

Lalala, Food is good

Lalala, Break-fast food

Lalala, Ce-re-al

Lalala, Ho-ney Nut

Lalala, Chee-ri-os

Lalala, Eat them up

Lalala, All gone now

Lalala, End this song

(He falls off the chair and laughs loudly at Himself) That's such a great song!! I should go and get it PUBLISHED!! YEAH! That's what I'll do!! As soon as I figure out why I AM THE BAD MAN! Ok...woo...ok...woo...ooookkk!!!!!! Umm, I forgot, HAHA!! *(He passes out and falls to the floor again, His journal slides off the table with Him and lands on His face with a dull thud)*

Owe...Last night was bad, I got drunk and passed out, and from the looks of it, I had fun, I really don't remember much; my head hurts.

It was for a good reason though, Joyce decided not to go out with me after all because, "you're too clingy, you're smothering me, we're not even boyfriend and girlfriend yet and I already need space." I get it now: girls don't want a bastard of a man that treats them bad and ignores them, but as soon as someone is being good to them and is nice and caring, I'm SMOTHERING them! Ahh, I see how it is, I should just cut off my penis with a dull meat cleaver, at least I would have an excuse for being so nice. That way, if she says I am being too "clingy," I can pull my pants down, "look! It's ok! I have no penis!" and maybe she'd understand why I was thinking with my lack-of-dick. I know I'm not perfect, but at least I'm not obsessed with getting into a girl's pants, in fact, I despise sex to a greater extent than most men do. I mean, who cares how it feels, I'm more entranced with the long-term consequences, say perhaps, ANOTHER HUMAN coming out of the deal! I can't stand little kids, they're like tiny undiplomatic versions of adults, only they break things that are expensive and pretty to look at. Not to mention the fact that I'm just a bit wacko myself, what business would I have being a parent? There are enough horrible parents out there to begin with – "Parents are no more than live-in sperm donors" – they don't need me adding to it. Also, there are the lies and the obligatory feelings, actions, and other such things that come with sexual relationships. "Four times means LOVE!" I really just don't want to be involved with that.

Luckily, we had been dating for about three weeks and that's not a very long time. Of course, I'm not sure if that's better or worse that she decided I was too "clingy" after such a short period of time. She could have at least told me that I was annoying her though, I mean, I asked her all the time to share her feelings about what I am and am not doing right. But no, she has to go and be all "you're the kind of guy I look for," and all this other BS, girls NEVER tell you how they REALLY feel! Don't they understand that we – men – can't understand hints, subtle, obvious, or blatant alike? If you want something, tell us, if you feel someway, tell us! It's insane in the membrane! Rrr, evil women people.

Whatever, I go through this every time I have a break-up, all three of them, and nothing ever changes, in fact, it just reaffirms my belief that everyone is the same. Come to think of it, all three of my girlfriends have said basically the same thing, and have broken-up with me for all the same reasons. It's annoying, but I'm not going to change myself just to get girls, I'll just have to find the right one...one who appreciates clingy.

I don't know, I guess I'm just upset because I was actually starting to think this one would work out for the best and it didn't. I was even letting my shields down, telling her about myself, my past, my future, all that stuff, and it just ended, like it meant nothing! That bothers me a lot...

Oh well, I better get off the floor, get dressed, get ready for school and all of that crap, can't have me missing school you know, perfect attendance and all that. I'm out.

11/20 7:48 a.m.

7
And then He Remembered

Holidays are coming soon.

Halloween decorations are now being sold in stores and it's not even Thanksgiving yet! I wouldn't be surprised if Christmas decorations were put out soon too, then New Years crap right after that. Such a mess, no one even really remembers the meanings of these holidays, just the consumable values of them. Like I've said before, the corporations just want you to buy more to fund their bonuses so that they can buy more and so on and so forth. I mean, what the hell is the point of a lot of money? All you do is buy more junk. Sure some toys are worth it for their entertainment value and what they can do to help you, but the majority of things like, new cars, new TVs, new new stuff is pointless. Stick with old school because it works just as well and probably entertains just as much. They don't even make toys anymore, just more virtual crap so that kids can sit on their butts, get fat, and think up strategies to kill their artificial enemies. Then people wonder why violent behavior is a constant and uninterrupted occurrence in our society.

I suppose this is the time of year where I get most spiteful about EVERYTHING because of the past events that surround the holidays of my life. It seems that every year the only holiday not ruined by someone, is Christmas (thank God) and Easter. Of course, that's probably because those are religious holidays and the majority of my family respect religion in one fanatical form or another. Instead though, nearly every other holiday – Thanksgiving especially – has been ripped apart in such a way that I no longer want to participate in these certain said holidays. Thanksgiving for example, was *always* one of the worst.

The day would usually begin slow for me, waking up around eleven A.M. and lethargically working my way through the house towards the smell of already cooking mashed potatoes, giblet stuffing, peas n' corn, turkey, and wonderful brown gravy to cover it all. Or so I wished it was such a peaceful awakening. Usually though, I awoke at the abrupt sound of my door swinging open and my mom yelling something at me about not helping and sleeping too much and dinner being ruined. These yells would then continue throughout the day, causing several fights among the three of us, until either the food was ready and the guests had arrived, or mom was intoxicated to the point of hyper stupidity. My mom has never been a drinker, but Thanksgiving is not only a day for celebration, but I day for alcohol induced calmness. Of course, after that she would begin her, "I suppose you don't like the food now because it's cold" routine or, "I'm sorry you hate it, but it's the only meal out of two that I make the whole year so you better enjoy it," pity crap. I always loved her food though, and made sure that she was aware of this fact. In my opinion my mom makes up for everything with her cooking and I wished that she had had time to do it more often, but that's ok, my mom being a busy person, never had much time to cook. Although, when she did cook, I could have gone without the yelling and the guilt trips. In fact, I wrote several poems one Thanksgiving and won a poetry contest for one of them. Strangely though, the poem I sent in was one of the shortest and worst that I had ever written, but apparently the company wanted money from me, so I guess that made it ok for them to plague off of my emotions and my amateur writing skills – assholes.

Halloween I've never really cared about, but also have never been allowed to take part in. My step-dad, being a religious and unusual man – whom I will not get into right now – did not enjoy the connotations involved with Halloween, and did not allow me take part in it. However, I've never been too fond of trying to kill my pancreas with candy, and enjoyed his alternative – dinner at a new restaurant. Because of these odd dinner experiences, I enjoy many different types of food: Japanese, Chinese, Cantonese, Taiwanese, Vietnamese, and the like -eses. It's all good food, and to this day, I enjoy visiting these restaurants as well as other's that Frank and Isaac have brought me to. I suppose Halloween never was a bad time, because before my step-dad came along, I dressed up as Robin Hood, Batman, and a Clown for my first few Halloween's, and thoroughly enjoyed each costume. Besides, I've never been too excited about bringing dead souls back to life and celebrating it with a band of naked witches and wizards and wiccans.

Anyway though, I can't think of the other holidays because either there aren't any or I just don't care to remember them. This year though, it looks like the three of us will be going over to Isaac's house to celebrate Thanksgiving. Accordingly, his family has a lot of fun; everyone sits in the kitchen, playing games, reminiscing, and or is at the table, all ready to eat before the food is even sizzling in its own juices. Also, the great thing about Isaac's family is that they don't invite many people; just him, his two sisters, whatever boyfriends or best friends they all have, and then of course his mother and father. They live in an old small house, but over the years, it has weathered large amounts of people and their heavy footfalls, so it should do nicely. Also, the food that his parents make is very much different then that of my mom's, so it should definitely be an interesting day to say the least.

Until then though, I suppose I will wait until the day of doom falls upon me before I write again. Luckily, it's on a Thursday, so I get a four-day weekend from school. It's exciting, but not, I think I'll just have macaroni and cheese – or not, we'll see. Good day – I think.

11/22 12:04 p.m.

Thanksgiving day, be afraid!

It is never a good idea to mix Frank, Isaac, and me with food, fun, and a less than stable house. Not only do we all eat people out of house n' home, but Frank and I enjoy breaking things that do not belong to us – a compulsive need. I suppose it all goes back to when I was a kid; explosions on TV and restlessness of the mind leads to 1) getting lots of toys 2) enjoying destruction 3) growing too old for those toys and 4) mixing gasoline, oil, and alcohol together to illegally commit acts of arson against those toys. Of course, it was always a fun display, especially when I blew Jonathan's eyebrows off. He had a unibrow anyway, so it was helpful, and they grew back several months later just fine. But that's got absolutely NOTHING to do with today.

It is Thanksgiving again and we all just got home from Isaac's house after an exciting day of eating and bowling. Actually, come to think of it, this is probably the best Thanksgiving I've had in a long time. In the institution, the day consisted of four hours of rounding up patients, sitting them down – hopefully dressed nicely or dressed at all – and feeding them several pounds of meat like substance. Then comes the best part, dehydrated mashed potatoes (Water Spuds), bread stuffing, paste gravy, and over steamed mixed vegetables. Such horribly great food. I remember one year when a patient became so disgruntled and disgusted at the food, he picked up the turkey shaped meat-mound and slammed it to the ground. Most of the patients cheered while others cried and pulled at the smashed Turkey, hoping for their share of the food before the five-second rule no longer applied. After the loud and rather disgusting feast, we would all be herded to the presentation room to watch a holiday movie; same one every year, "Thanks to us all." Old movie, bad actors, strange plot, but good nonetheless. I enjoyed it the first time, but slept every year after. I suppose the idea of watching the same movie once a year was not the problem, but more so that we were forced to, and that the institution did not care enough to buy another cheap Thanksgiving video for us live-in patients. Oh well, it was but two hours of my life wasted in comparison of the many other's used.

This year though, Thanksgiving was very much different than it ever has been. This year, there was no screaming and yelling and inane whining and complaining about kitchen space and lethargic, unhelpful males. Nor was it a routine day of eating food with the simple instructions of, "just add water." No, today was good. The three of us got to Isaac's house late in the afternoon, and right away were greeted by his father, mother, dog, and sisters. They all seemed happy to see us, and as usual, we were happy to see them. Throughout the years, his family has always been the most outgoing/nicest people I've ever known. Isaac's sister took me to my first concert, let me set her hand on fire, and got me interested in going to college (unfortunate that I was never able to). I enjoy his family because they are fun people: unafraid to say what they think, unafraid to do what they want, and unafraid...of anything, so it seems. Eh, well, they're cool. We had a meal, very different from the food that the hospital and my mom used to make. Their turkey was real, but smaller and not as moist as my mom's was. Luckily though, I enjoy dark meat (must be part of being left-handed), so mine was very much more moist than everyone else's was. They also made steamed green beans, *real* mashed potatoes, stuffing, thick brown gravy, and canned cranberry sauce (the BEST). I enjoyed the meal to the extent of four helpings; I can no longer walk without my stomach making sloshing noises, I love it. After we finished, we all sat at the table for about an hour, talking about everyone's latest adventures in the world and about old times – I enjoy nostalgia, it tickles.

Finally, the table was clear, the dishes washed, and the kids ready to play. I sat down at the table, assuming we were going to play Monopoly or something, but when I turned around, everyone was putting on their shoes and coats and was heading for the door. I followed, and some time later, ended up at a bowling ally. I can't bowl but it was fun anyway. I bowled a sixty-two, Frank bowled a two forty-two, and Isaac bowled a two eighty-eight. They used to be on a league and both learned how to bowl insanely well. I hate bowling, I enjoy Hockey, watching and playing.

So anyway, nothing really big or important happened this year except that over a million people gave thanks to their God(s), their country, their job, or themselves, and in some cases, to paperwork and corporations. Thanksgiving luckily, is one of the few big holidays that does not involve buying gifts. So, I discontinue my boycott of the holiday, and have decided that it is in fact a good day because only grocery stores profit. But I must go because I'm bored, good day!

11/25 9:45 p.m.

School.

Some people call it a prison, some call it heaven, some say it's no big deal, and the rest understand that it is a necessary evil. However, very few people understand that it takes a certain attitude to appreciate school, despite the label that they give it.

As I walk through the halls, I hear many people complain about the way the school is run, about their teachers, about the administration, rules, and everything else that the school is. I don't think they understand that, even though they do not know everything, without school, they would know absolutely nothing. I'm exaggerating of course, because there are things learned through osmosis, and there is knowledge gained through experience as well, but for the most part they would know nothing more than trivial tasks and clichés. Of course, I also believe that there are more people that *do* understand and appreciate school, but complain anyway because it is what they are expected to do. I suppose, someone who enjoys something as simple and irritating as school, *must* be crazy, anal, a suck-up, or just plane stupid, for the majority of people are content with the fact that they know nothing and do nothing to change this.

So, I guess I'm a stupid-plane-crazy-anal-suck-up. For, I enjoy the idea of learning as much as possible in a short period of time. I find that there are a great many new things and experiences and bits of knowledge in the world that I will never know without school. Obviously, there are the things that I really couldn't care less about, but there are also a great many things that I am interested in – philosophy, history, math, music, etc. Oh well though, I guess there's no way I can really spread my strange liking for school to the rest of the student body, so I'll keep this idea to myself.

Recently, I've found myself increasingly irritable because of the things people say around and to me. People think they're so special when they notice things and find it necessary to confirm or brag their findings. Several people, for example, have noticed that I am a quiet person, and, being loud themselves, have decided to make it their quest in life to find out why I'm so quiet. Of course, they can't just come to me quietly and ask, "why are you so quiet?" Instead, they make assumptions and accusations, attempt to analyze me, and then startlingly profess their findings to the world. Now this in itself, is not the worst thing in the world, but the conclusions that they come to are rather off and annoying. Why, just yesterday, someone came up to me offering consolation for my loss. As far as I know, I have not lost anything or anyone, although I did lose a sock in the wash, I doubt seriously that they knew that. I remained quiet until they had apologized for bothering me, attempted to make phony conversation, and finally left. After the person left though, I turned to my friend Kevin and continued our conversation about the difference between hot dogs and bologna. He thinks hot dogs have a higher manufacturing standard than bologna, whereas I've actually been inside both factories, and know that they allow up to four rats to fall in per vat of meat mix. However, I'm not sure the allowed amount of bugs, droppings, and the like, so in that case, he might be right. But that's got nothing to do with the price of gas.

Anyway though, school is fun, but is becoming increasingly stressful and annoying because of the people and the work involved with it. I am unsure how I feel today because I am rather exhausted mentally and physically. I have a lot of things I've got to get done this week with the guys, with school, with work, and for myself, so I probably won't write until things calm down or get worse. I'm hoping for the calm, but if things continue this way, I will be writing the latter entry. I must go, it's time for work, and I'm still in my underwear. Long day.

11/30 3:12 p.m.

Today was confusing to say the least.

I'm scared, stressed out, and I fear a repeat of the past. Recently I've been remembering a lot of things about my past: "Pre-Journal" times, what led up to and secured my admittance to the institution, and because I've never written it down, maybe I will today

It all started about five years ago, around the same time of year, when I started hearing the "voices" in my head. However, these are not the voices of schizophrenia – which was what I was original diagnosed with – but instead, is my inner monologue talking so quickly and incoherently, that it sounds like many people having a party in my mind. Hmm, that could be fun,

Paranoid Schizophrenic

Fiendish plans of conspiracy be
Against us all, but mostly me
Lingering wonders of ethereal thought
Thinking of things that I should not
Confusion, it's horrid, insipid, and placid
All at once, a magic delusion
None be true to you, then who?
My mind still wanders yonder it saunters
All this fright, these millions of choices
To conclude at this; I'm hearing more voices

Hehehe…Anyway, This caused headaches and also caused me to murmur, babble, and pace in the effort of calming myself. Also, it caused stress, which was what the *original* stress was caused by, thus creating a vicious cycle. I tried many things to stop it, became angry beyond reason, and in a horrible attempt to stop it all, became increasingly violent. This was not good for many reasons, which I will explain soon, but I must record, that I was never violent prior to that time. In fact, I was quite opposite.

Stress. It's all caused by stress, hell, what isn't caused by stress nowadays? Accordingly to "Psi Magazine," seventy-eight percent of all trauma and or mental anxiety, and overall life problems, are caused by stress on the job, at home, or at school. The rest of it is hereditary or caused by traumatizing events. I have never been able to handle most types of stress in my life, especially that which is created by other people, for I try to do anything and almost everything on my own. Then, when people impede or interrupt my work or any other number of things related to people, I become stressed. To cut a longer story long, many things built up all at once and I lashed out, becoming violent towards people that I love.

One reason I was in the institution for so long is because I did not have much confidence in myself, save for my generally annoying superiority complex and constant, irrational urge to beat certain said people with large, shinny, blunt objects. These are the events that secured my admittance into the institution.

I was talking to Frank on the phone like I usually did everyday while my mom yelled at me from another room, and like every other day, I closed and locked the door to my room and ignored her. Normally, it would have been like any other day, but like I said, I was stressed much more than usual, for many things had hit the fan and splattered. I always used to imagine things I could do to my mom to shut her up, but never considered doing them with a final degree of seriousness. This time however, she was pushing me much too far and Frank was being slightly annoying, but understanding in his own strange, Asian sort of way. I'm not sure what happened to push me over the edge, but from what I can remember, and from what I've heard from witnesses and victims, goes something like this:

145

My adrenaline began to pump, so I threw the phone across the room, thus breaking it into several unsalvageable parts.   I went to my closet and picked up my engraved Louisville Slugger, ripped open the door, putting a hole in the wall with the doorknob, and proceeded to find my mom. When I found her she was ranting about something stupid I'm sure, and I told her, in not so nice a way, to shut up. When she mocked my threat I gave her one last chance to shut up, but she wouldn't.   Instead, she came at me in quick motion, so I shattered her arm (according to X-rays). I warned her again and said that next time I wouldn't be so nice as to hit her arm, and as she broke down to cry on the floor in pain, I walked back to my room to put the phone back together so that I could finish my conversation with Frank. The dying animal sounds from below eventually subsided and soon there was a knock at the front door and the sound of footfalls on the stairs. I turned around from my desk and vain attempt at phone repair to find two police officers standing in my doorway, both with their hands by their guns. I answered their questions incoherently with maniacal laughter and an expression of relief, satisfaction, disdain, and madness.   After a week of questionnaires, evaluations, a hearing, and other such garbage of the related nature, I was placed into the Mental Health Ward, where I stayed for the remainder of my teenage life, and on until one year after legal drinking age.

Today I realized that, although I *have* gotten better, not that much has really changed, I never really learned how to deal with stress while I was in the institution because I was never really under any *real* stress.   Therefore, without experience to guide me, I learned nothing more than what Dr. Shutz and Cole told me. However much they did say though, is perhaps now, what is helping me to keep my sanity.

Presently, community college is getting harder than I expected now that we're nearing the second semester. My grades are slipping more than I personally allow them to, and I lost my job at 22-Hour Fitness yesterday because someone complained, saying that I didn't know what I was talking about and hurt them. I think the idiot just didn't want to try my rigorous workout routine and got hurt just to be a jerk. But whatever, that's not the point, the point is I can't pay the rent now and the guys might kick me out because of it, especially since Frank would do it just to be a jerk. For the same reason, money, I wasn't able to find or afford a good car, so I will still be using the bus for my travel, which will probably be limited anyway. The computer isn't working well so I can't connect to Virtual Net to check my mail and or communicate with my inspirational Canadian friend BCB. Also, my family wants to see me, I really don't like them much, but I guess I could live with it, except that my mom is coming to visit too, because a certain roommate thought it would be nice to invite her to dinner. So, as I said above, the "voices" are coming back, and I think that I might have to hide in the closet and rock until it all goes away or perhaps I'll sleep or write –forever. Who knows maybe something good will come out of all of this…wonder what it'll be. Anyway, I'm going to go do something that is neither interesting nor noteworthy, and I don't even really know what that something is. Perhaps I'll sulk, or maybe I'll just sit and stare at the wall, either way it's up to probability. Long day.

12/7 11:28 p.m.

Mental Hospital; the early years.

After I wrote my last entry, I started thinking a lot about the events that took place surrounding and following my admittance to the institution. In fact, I've been thinking about the entire three years prior to my journal, that I'm calling the, "Pre-Journal" years. I suppose, that it is an understatement to say that I did not change much at all, because in fact, I changed a LOT, it's just that, as I always say, life is a circle, so it's only irrationally logical that I start having problems again right now.

I don't remember ever being diagnosed with a particular disorder, but instead many small ones that created the larger chunk of my problem(s). For all intents and purposes I was classified as Paranoid with violent tendencies, and was put on Ward One, which is for people with mild disorders and problems that do not generally require medication unless for mood disorders or as temporary inhibitors. My ward was considered lower security than the rest, and the people on it were generally allowed many more privileges than the people on other Wards. These Wards generally consisted of people that required daily restraints, Valium, or other such tranquilizers, barbiturates, sedatives and the like "fun drugs." Then finally there was the last ward, which we all called the "Storage Ward," it is reserved for the incurable patients, such as Schizophrenics and catatonics.

Anyway though, I am also to be a highly Schizoid, Schizotypal, Histrionic, Obsessive (but not compulsive) person. Luckily, these mood disorders are considered small when by themselves and together, because the lot of them generally overlap in their definitions and fluctuate in the same way that my moods do. My physical health, luckily, has always been excellent, so I am not allergic to any medications and never required special attention from any of the behemoth nurses or orderlies.

I remember my first day there, I still had that mad, satisfied glow about me despite everything that had happened between breaking my mom's arm and stepping foot into the place that I, at the time, considered my future forever-home. I scanned the lobby and adjacent rooms and committed them to memory so that I could have mental blueprints of as much of the building as possible. Now all I remember is the sick, industrial yellow color of the brick walls, similar to that of my old schools. I was introduced to Dr. Shutz and his sincere smile, the one I would see many more times from that point on. He attempted to start a conversation with me, but I said very little, in fact, I said very little to him or anyone else I did not know for the next two years. That was my first mistake. He gave me a tour of Ward One, and by the end of the tour I was cold with nervousness; too many people, too much confinement, too much or too little of all the wrong things and to say the least, I was scared. I knew then that I had made a mistake, but still did not regret nor feel remorse for what I had done, and felt stubbornly content with the consequences of my actions, no matter how wrong those actions were.

The first year it seems took the longest, nearly ten years. I spoke to very few people and when I did, it was only because I needed something: directions, information, etc. I did not vent; I only ranted and raved to myself and whoever else was in the area. I was generally ignored and feared, for I was at the peak of my physical strength and was capable of melting metal with my demonic stare. Also, I had frequent appointments with Dr. Shutz, the majority of which ended early and were counterproductive. I was a stubborn bastard and would answer his questions contradictorily, incoherently, or with two words or less. I was not there to be helped, I was there to be caged up from society – I thought. In fact, during the first year, the only productive thing I did was workout in my room, find my corner to sit and watch from, eat, sleep, clean when requested, and participate as little as possible during Ward field trips and group activities. I thought I was the big tough guy that didn't need anyone or anything. I was visited frequently by family and friends and each time they came I would lie, telling them how much progress I was making, that I would get out soon, and would truthfully tell them how much I missed them.

The second year was the same, except that I had learned the rhythm of daily events and how to interact safely with each person that was there for longer than six months. I continued to avoid Dr. Shutz's questioning, but no longer gave two word answers. In fact, I filled in our hours with loads of trivial information about friends, family, and things that I had read that week, month, or year. In my own manipulative way, I hoped that my excited talk would lead him to believe that I was getting better. I found out later though, that he knew exactly what I was doing and did not buy it for even a minute. Instead, he was waiting for me to open up about *myself*, but did not sense I would. So, he adjusted my appointments so that they were less frequent, giving me time to think more about our conversations, and at the same time, letting him take care of the increasing patient population more adequately.

The middle of the second year finally marked noticeable change. Visits from friends and family took a sudden drop. It took me a while to notice, but after my eighteenth birthday, very few people came to see me anymore. For the very first time I was actually alone and I was deathly aware and afraid of it. I suppose for the first couple years I considered the whole deal a game, never really taking it seriously and never really letting it sink in that, "HEY! You're in a mental hospital moron!" I began thinking more seriously about my situation, but again was thinking counterproductively and was depressing myself more often than not with thoughts of helplessness and the like emotions. I, for the first time, had an entire hour long session with the Doc about only myself, using full sentences, complex analysis (as far as I can provide of myself), and explanations of my feelings, thoughts, and behaviors. Dr. Shutz said that he was proud and that I had made a medium sized breakthrough, but however was still missing the big picture. I agreed, but still was not ready for

HUGE breakthroughs, only small ones, and wasn't even sure what the "big picture" was. I began writing poetry again to express myself more thoroughly, but failed miserably and only wrote many replications of my first "Alone" poem. No matter though, they are all in a large folder filled with hundreds of other poems and files, locked away in some gigantic filing cabinet where no one will ever see them. Luckily, I was still receiving encouragement from my dad and other people through mail and random visits; they are what kept me alive.

These things, among violent bouts, massive bipolar like mood swings, hours of boredom, sitting, thinking, rocking, avoiding, and many other negative, horrible, inane things of this nature, filled the first two years and did not accomplish much of anything. In fact, they set me back, but with Dr. Shutz's profundity, humanistic qualities, and constant annoying encouragement, I slowly worked my way towards year three.

By the third year, my self-esteem had taken a drop and the only thing I had self-respect for was my large vocabulary, which, was no longer even being used. The only person I talked to was Dr. Shutz, and by then I considered him a friend and no longer felt the need to impress him with big words. Luckily though, I had been talking about myself more and had finally admitted to him what had gotten me there in the first place, regardless of the fact that I knew he already knew. His encouragement was what kept the little bit of confidence I had left, but was still not enough to make me think I was good enough for even a bed, let alone release. At about that time, Dr. Shutz saw that all things had been exhausted as far as talking and therapy techniques were concerned, so he turned to pharmaceuticals. I don't remember what any of them were called, but I know they were color coded, and that I only tried three different ones. For the fact that the first two did not work, he suggested that I write a journal and take the new third pill. The rest is recorded history, because for the next year, I changed exponentially.

That's the short version. The long version would be a book, so I think I'll retire to my bed before I actually write one, good morning...crap I have school no time for sleep. Bad morning.

12/8 6:02 a.m.

My mom.

She's coming over later today to have dinner with us, nothing special, Frank is a decent cook – better than Isaac or me – so he will be making white rice, Korean sushi, chow mein, and lemon chicken for us all. His lemon chicken is about the best I've ever had and could kill – in a good way – anyone for it because it's so delicious.

I don't know what to expect, because the last time I saw her, my perception was on the angry side to say the least and now it's on the stressed side, thus making me ready to snap in a more subtle way than before. Either way though, I'm not sure what will happen, I'm willing to bet that, for the first hour or so everyone will speak with awkwardness in their voice, skimming over any really deep topics; school, weather, news, work, and maybe politics. Of course, during dinner, someone will bring up something touchy and it will cause my mom to get defensive, then someone will take that defensiveness personally, defend their position and somehow the conversation will erupt into something unsavory. Finally, we will all (meaning mom and I) be arguing about something that had nothing to do with the original conversation and it will probably have to do with me not visiting, loving, caring, or listening to her, and might possibly be all of them at once. If we're lucky though, we can get her tipsy and she'll suddenly become a much easier person to deal with.

On the other hand, I could be totally wrong, but I seriously doubt that, people don't change easily or quickly, do they? Well, I need to get ready, so I'll write about what happens later. Good luck.

12/9 9:58 a.m.

A dinner gone awry.

Isaac answered the door when my mom arrived because I was hiding in my room. I had been building up my confidence, calming myself, clearing my mind and praying – which I haven't done for many years. After she walked in I become startlingly nervous, and the sound of Frank yelling about the food being almost ready, made me jump.

After we all sat done to eat – exquisite food – there was an awkward silence – first of eight from my count – however, conversation picked up, and for almost an hour, all was good. I think Isaac felt he was on a roll today because he started a new topic. It was, however, the "dreaded topic," both Frank and I knew it, for we both know what happens when you ask my mom how she's doing. We both shot a glance, telling him to quickly change the subject, but he did not understand and instead encouraged her to continue. At first though, she shoved it off and only told us some simple things, but suddenly remembered her health and began speaking spitefully about her health and about the people that had upset her at work, in stores, or on the road that week. At first, we all were interested because we all enjoy the flaws of others, human nature dictates that, but soon thereafter, we all became rather annoyed that she wouldn't stop. I tried to hurry her story along with an "ok mom," but I was ignored and her story continued.

Strangely though, before we all were about to blank out and block out, she stopped, so naturally I asked if she was ok.

She said that she was ok and continued saying, "I'm probably boring you guys, tell me how life's been treating *you* all!" ALL of us were taken aback and again there was another awkward silence. I've never seen this in my mom and neither has any of the rest of us – sudden genuine interest in someone else's life above her own. Almost at once, we all began talking about our current life situations, only to stumble over each other and laugh. She too laughed, genuinely, and again I was taken aback. We decided to take turns, and during the next hour, we all learned something about each other's daily lives and interactions that we had not known before. In a scary sort of way, it was enjoyable, filled with laughter, which continued throughout the night as we played ten thousand, a dice game that I haven't played since I was in Kentucky with Grandma Edna. May she rest in peace and her soul in heaven, for it is where she belongs, the most wonderful, cute, jealous little old lady in the world.

After several long games of ten thousand, the night ended and the morning began, but for the guys and I it was just getting late, but for my mom, it was beyond late and she was exhausted. We all offered to give her a ride home, but she refused each time with, "such nice boys, I'm ok." I walked her to her car, for I was in a very good mood. I said bye and much to my surprise she grabbed on to me and...hugged me. I froze stiff as a board – natural reaction – but soon relaxed and hugged her back nervously. She began to cry softly and whispered "sorry" into my ear. The last awkward silence of the night followed as my mind spun to a stop. I had no idea what to say or do, for this was the most unprecedented, unexpected, thing to happen EVER in my life, ESEPCIALLY with my mom. I remained silent even as she searched my eyes and my soul for a response. She seemed satisfied with what she found, because she smiled at me, got into her car, and drove away. I was an expressionless statue for several minutes;

only my eyes blinked enough to stop the sting of the cold breeze.

Right now, I still don't know what to think, and perhaps I won't for a while, this will take much time to even understand or make sense of, for it is not at all what I expected to have happen. I suppose I should call her or something…who knows, I'll talk to Jane about it, ask her what to think, but right now I'm dead tired and am running out of brain energy, so I will fall asleep watching and making-fun of infomercials with the guys. Strange night.

12/11 4:11 a.m.

Just odd things, nothing really important – things I notice.

It turns out my family can't make it out here because they have some big event to plan, I don't know what though because Isaac didn't write the message down, but I know it's something important and boring. Besides, I've been trying to keep my schedule thin so that I don't flip, which is strange because I've been reading a few of my recent entries and I sound strangely calm in all of them, even though I don't feel calm at all. In fact, I've been quite hyper recently, but I suppose that's more difficult to display on paper without being incoherent, so in a way, I guess my journal is helping me to stay sane once again.

I talked to Jane about what happened with my mom and she's *more* afraid of her now than she ever was before. In seriousness though she said that I should call her and start out by asking what she is sorry about. Then, as the conversation progresses, I should apologize too. I wasn't at first sure what I had to apologize for until Jane told me to think about it, then I remembered the whole, smashing her arm thing and the constant hostility from that time forward and decided that Jane was right. So! I suppose that's what I'll have to do, but not now, I'm still not ready to make a step like that with my mom.

Speaking of Jane, wow, I haven't talked to her in a long time, many things have happened with her, well, about as far as many things go with Jane. She spends most of her time watching TV, playing on the net, and going to parties with drunks, druggies, and horny men, all things that she said she'd never do. I find it interesting how much Jane has changed, but then, she hates "sameness," so it's not so surprising, I just never thought she would be so promiscuous and worldly. That's fine though because she's still a good kid, doesn't do any illegal drugs – a phrase which becomes less and less significant as the years go by – and she knows the difference between reality, TV, and Reality TV. I always worry about her though; she drives like a maniac and takes stupid risks sometimes so that she can "experience life to the fullest." Oh well, as long she is having fun it's not really my place to say or do anything to the contrary.

For now I remain jobless, but the guys have agreed to let me stay, how nice. I would only hope that my two best friends in the world would let my stay in the only place I can call home. They jokingly said that if push comes to shove, out the door that is, I could live with my mom. I didn't find that funny whether her attitude has changed or not.

I'm really tired today, I keep falling asleep in math class, and today just realized that I am passing the class with a D-, which means that I am for sure going to need to start staying awake and might even need a tutor. Maybe I'll catch up on my sleep in computer class because I'm passing it with an A+, it's interesting, what can I say. Of course, there's always the last ditch alternative, which is, go to sleep earlier than one or two A.M., but that would involve a massive sleep schedule change. Heh, maybe I'll try that, "last ditch alternative," first? Probably a good idea.

Speaking of funny stupid things, I was somewhere yesterday, not sure where, don't remember and don't care, and I noticed a funny thing about people. People talk to pets as if their pets are people too. It's a very common and strange occurrence and I've always seen it, never really paid attention to it, and in the back of my head, have always wondered how and why people form such emotional bonds with their pets. I mean, no offense, but pets are just small, four-legged creatures with primitive brains and have the life span of a toaster. Granted they are very intelligent creatures that can learn and show emotion at time, but with all that, they can't even carry on conversations with people. Sadly, if I can't have a conversation with someone or something they become nothing at all or at the most become purely entertainment (this is how TV works). I suppose I just have a problem with forming a relationship with anyone or anything that I can't talk to and have it talk back, which is where, I suppose, my biggest REAL problem with God is. Anyway, pets are fun, but if I were to ever own one, I don't think I would talk to it very often unless I taught it commands and how to do my homework. Of course, pets are easier than kids, so who knows, maybe I would get one if it meant I would be responsible for it instead of a kid – try passing that one off on your wife.

Oi, even thinking about having a kid makes my head hurt. It's so difficult now-a-days trying to bring your kids up the right way. It used to be that you could just stick them in front of the TV until they were thirteen years old and they'd be just fine, but now, you've got to nurture them and like, do other stuff with them – eww. Of course, there are some houses (for extraordinarily rich people) that have many automated machines and time-saver devices, much like the houses in Ray Bradbury's <u>Fahrenheit 451</u>, but those are rare. It seems that kids learn everything important in life before the parents ever get a chance to teach it to them. Generally, this would be a good thing, but since what they learn is more often than not wrong, it makes it just a tad bit more difficult for the parents. But then, on the other side of the coin, parents of bad parents that were brought up the same way kids are brought up now, turn out to be horrible parents. They teach kids twisted morals about promiscuity being good, disrespect being acceptable, and deplorable behavior being allowed, either through example or by not teaching them the opposite. It seems that Frank, Isaac, and I are the only remaining "good fellas," in the world, or so I like to believe. Heh, I remember that we used to all say that a lot, that we would be the only ones left after a World War (along with three good females) and that we would all be responsible for repopulating the world. But because TV would survive through satellites and our children would see us all having sex on a regular and uninterrupted basis (to repopulate of course), they would take example and eventually turn out to be exactly like the previous generations. However long that might take, it would still be the outcome because the world is a never ending circle and rerun of itself, the only thing that really ever changes is the tools we use to make and destroy each other and the names of the people that do the creating and destroying.

Speaking of satellites and technology, I've heard about this really awesome new cell phone. It's implanted into your brain, very tiny receiver type dealio, and you can just THINK to the person. About one thousand dollars depending on the options you get on it, plus it's still in it's early stages of development so there's still a lot of kinks to work out. Most of the problems are caused because the average human mind can not think clearly for a long enough time to think solely about one phone number or person and then talk to them with one string of thought. However, if you can get it to call, the NeuroCell can single out the certain inner monologue you want to use for talking to the person. I think the reason it has the problem with the other part is because: number memory is on a different side and is accessed by several different parts of the brain than the "inner monologue side" is. Anyway, I hate cell phones, but I still thought it was interesting and noteworthy seeing since it's part of what's going on in my world, and if anyone were to ever be bored enough to find my notebook, then actually read it, they might want to know what was going on in the world at the time.

Anyway, it's early in the morning again, so I'm going to bed, good night, short day, long week.

12/13 1:26 a.m.

Sudden turn for the worse.

Last week was surprisingly good, and this week was surprisingly bad! See, you would think visits from mom, no money, and failing classes would upset me, but no, it just puts me into a creepy calm state, but this time I'm just a BIT more upset! I don't even really know why, it's just stupid little things again, nothing REALLY big actually happened!

I've been getting more sleep and am now staying awake in all my classes; this depletes more energy faster than I thought. I get home and only have time to go on the net for a while and do my homework, except yesterday, I forgot to write an entire essay for English and didn't study for a test in Government. I hereby hate government now because I failed my first test. Normally, I do pretty well in that class, but this time I just failed it, had NO clue what it was even talking about. Oh well that sucks, guess I'll have to stay up again and do extra work or something.

Of course, this doesn't help much with my dwindling social life, the one that's been dwindling ever since the beginning of the month. Now though, it's cutting into my time with the guys, I've had to refuse their offers to go out several times already, I hope they don't take it personally.

Also, Jane is mad at me because I never called to tell her about what happened with my mom, also, when she called I was short with her because I was grouchy (she had woken me up) and had nothing new to report to her. I think I hung-up on her, which, wouldn't be the first time...more like the second time. Also, today I was having a conversation with one of my neighbors about perception of craziness or something like that and some jock overheard me talking about me being in a mental hospital. I hope he doesn't go blab about that, because as much as I don't care, I care. Especially if it's a big, dumb jock. Oh well, whatever, I doubt anything will come of it.

Anyway, I'm generally in a grouchy mood, my sleep schedule has been fluctuating a LOT lately, at least before I was always going to bed within the same hour. Now, I'm taking afternoon naps, eating at strange times, losing my memory, and being lazy; haven't worked out in a long time either, that probably has affected my general state of being too.

Oh well, I'm off too bed. Good...whatever time it is.

12/15

I'm pissed.

You know what? I'm not just mad, I'm freakin' pissed off, I was really looking forward to sitting down and watching Jane open her presents and do the birthday thing with just the two of us. But no! If she can't be fuckin' patient and wait one hour, then that's just too damned bad! She knows damn well that I have a lot of things to do, and if I can't call right away or come over at a moment's notice then that's just too bad! And if she's mad at me I'm sorry, but this is just bullshit! Damn it! Why can't this be a good day!?

(He jabs the pen through several pages in the notebook, sees what He's done, becomes angrier, throws the notebook across the room

and is about to cry, but at the last second stands up and pouts off to His room to scream some more.)

Limbo.

I don't know if I want today to end right now, or go on forever. I don't know if I want to go to school now, or never...that should be a poem...maybe it will be one of these days...oh well whatever.

I think I'm just tired, or bored, or something, because I don't want today to end, because it was a neutral day for one and two because I don't want tomorrow to start, that will just mean going to school and actually doing stuff and who knows what kind of good or bad variables will show up! Oh well.

"Hey NUT!" mocks a large, behemoth like football player, "I heard that you're from a NUT house!"

"Maybe I am, what the hell business is it of yours?"

"Oh nothing, I just thought maybe I'd see if the rumors were true!" he continues, snickering and mocking.

Rolling His eyes, He shifts to a defensive stance, "What the HELL do you care?"

"Ooo, getting a little touchy aren't we? So, is it true, are you a NUT!?"

Irritated, "I don't know about you, but I am getting a bit touchy...And yes I have been in an institution."

"HA! I knew it! You're a psycho aren't you! What'd you do FREAK!?" his volume increases annoyingly.

"As a matter of fact, I nearly killed my mother, because I have, 'violent tendencies,' and it's best that you don't test me today! Get me!?"

Mockingly, "Ohh, does that mean you're going to hurt me!? Huh little boy, what you gonna do?" at that, the jock begins making annoying cooing noises.

"Shut up..." He decides to hell with it and starts walking away. But the idiot jock does not stop his incessant noises and begins

to walk after him. That's when the jock makes a dumber mistake. He grabs at the Nut, touching His back and suddenly the jock's arm is in a lock that could easily be used to break that arm. Instead of backing off though, the jock cackles – his final mistake. With two quick, deft movements, the jock is on the ground with his arm and wrist immobilized, a thumb pressed firmly into his esophagus, and a knee in his diaphragm.

"LISTEN HERE KID! DO NOT SCREW WITH ME, I am NOT a nice person, ESPECIALLY when YOU feel the need to TOUCH ME...GET ME SNAPPLE!?"

The jock attempts to ignore the threat but suddenly feels his wrist begin to give in to the pressure.

"I am FASTER AND SMARTER THAN YOU and I KNOW how to kill you...NOW! Do you get me, KID!?"

As his breathing becomes labored, he gets the hint. He nods his head, then after a few seconds, the knee lifts, the thumb releases, and his wrist relaxes. There is a sudden pat on his cheek, or perhaps a slap, he could not tell, for his face is numb. The jock watches the Nut stand up, straighten his shirt slowly and precisely, then walk away. The jock lay there for a few moments gathering himself, then stands and walks away as well, seemingly unbothered by the events that have just transpired.

Today I did something bad.

Today I reverted to my caveman instincts, instead of being intelligent about something I became violent. I'm not just talking about banging a rock against the peanut butter jar to open it, I mean, I injured someone.

One thing I can't tolerate is ignorant, disrespectful people, especially those of which who are arrogant and convinced that they actually know what they're talking about, and that find it necessary to *attempt* to make others look bad in the process. Today, I guess I just wasn't in a tolerant mood. Of course, it was his own doing; he should have never touched me. It's one thing to mock me and make-fun of my past because I really don't care, in fact, I walked away from him at first. But when he decided to *touch* me, he made a HUGE mistake. I mean, some stupid jock, hearing rumors (true ones) about me being in the institution, and then trying to make-fun of me for it!? What kind of CRAP is that? The things idiots do to feel big n' special. The funny thing is though, he was stronger than I am, and I still flattened him to the ground with my knee in his stomach, thumb in his throat, and wrist locked. Something I learned way back in the day, that if I twist someone's wrist just right, I can push it down and crush his humorous. I don't think I did that to this guy, but I did put enough pressure on it to make it sore for a few days.

Luckily though, I feel better, and released a lot of stress, about as good as masturbation, only it was violence! That's so sad, the two of them go hand in hand, no pun intended. Anyway, I don't feel like going into details, it all happened fast and it's over now so who cares, I just hope I don't get into trouble for it. No, I doubt he'll tell anyone that he got his butt kicked by someone smaller than him, smarter, faster, and crazier too.

Dr. Shutz would NOT be very proud, but who cares, at least I know why I was in the institution now – they should have "violent, tension release therapy." Wait, they do, it's when you beat people with foam bats. Oh well, it looks like I need to work on my control again. At least I've gotten better, I used to be much worse, would do things like that to people just for looking at me funny in the hospital. But, I must go; I have much studying to do. The End.

12/17 4:30 p.m.

...Actually, I just remembered a time when I did that during one of the first years I was in the institution. I did that to someone during group – I tried group once; it didn't work. I don't remember what was wrong with him, but I remember that he kept making fun of me and everyone else. At that time though, I was really pissed off, so I started choking him to death because he wouldn't shut up and wouldn't stop repeating people like a parrot. He didn't even really attack me, it was just his annoying tone of voice, and irritating mocking that bothered me so much. When everyone saw me choking him it created a mess in group and everyone started making noise, copying me, and whatever other chaos you could possibly imagine. Several orderlies pulled me off, and just like every other time that happened (I'm sure there were other instances I can't remember) I ended up in solitary confinement. It's set backs like that that make me curl up into my bubble...heh, the proverbial one, not the sugar one.

Eureka!

I think I've found out the nice way of explaining why people are so stupid! Aaron and I have been finding more compelling evidence to support the idea that people are sheep. And along with that, we've also found that people like him, George, and me (and others that are aware of the sheep factor) must be the herding dogs. Sadly though, the one's that take advantage of the "sheep," are wolves.

Sheep are those people whom buy into propaganda, are gullible, talk to their pets, and enjoy pop music and odd shaped furniture. They are the people that do not think for themselves, but instead easily except the things of the world that really don't make much sense if looked at logically. They are the ones that get themselves high, stoned, or drunk so that they don't have to do something or so that they don't have to face reality. They are the people that take up the majority of the world population.

Herding dogs...hold on I'm hungry...Mmm, I love Cinnamon Butter Crème Cake! Anyway, the herding dogs are the people that are aware of the sheepliness of people and try to avoid being like that themselves. They do this by creating their own personal opinions on things, doing/buying what they want, not what they're told to through propaganda, and by thinking, listening, caring, and using logic.

Wolves of course, are the people that start large companies and take advantage of the sheep through commercials, consumables, and other such demanding ideas, products, services, and appearances. Wolves take advantage of most everyone and are the true demons of this planet. Wolves are bad for everyone's health, including mine, because even the dogs get hurt/sucked into the lies and propaganda of the wolves.

Anyway, to the point, I think that everyone is born with the instinctual need to learn, grow, and become dogs. Some of us, however, have that need satisfied on a constant and regular basis from the beginning of our lives, therefore we learn more easily in our futures. Unfortunately though, there are others whom are not nurtured properly or do not learn at all and never develop the need to learn/the neural and psychological connections for comprehension. These two things are what separate the different parts of the Belle Curve and everything in between. It all depends on the different levels of parenting and education that person receives. If a child's questions are answered correctly, with detail, they will grow, and hopefully become curious on their own – we are all curious by nature – thus learn to become dogs. When the opposite upbringing occurs, you get the Sheep Factor. This is why I will not be a parent, because I have NO idea when and when not to answer these questions correctly etc., it's way too difficult.

Finally, with the increasing trend of bad parenting (to coin a phrase "Now-a-days, there is no such thing as good parents, just live-in sperm donors"), the need for learning and knowledge is steadily decreasing into a pit of nothingness. So much so, that any self-respecting chimpanzee with a lab coat could get through the world with little to no trouble. Of course, that poor chimpanzee would probably commit suicide because he would not be capable of living up to our social standards, and would be considered an outcast because of his hairiness and choice of clothing (The lab coat).

Therefore, I conclude that the few of us left that are aware of these problems, should all become teachers, and should try to repopulate the world with enlightened people. And, on a more drastic note, anyone who shows blatant stupidity in the face of obviousness should be shot in the crotch with an x-ray gun so that they are unable to reproduce.

12/18 7:22 p.m.

Today was thought provoking.

I was sleepy today, again, and fell asleep as soon as I sat down in the computer chair. While sleeping, I had a weird dream, like I sometimes do, that made me think. My dream was sort of a wake-up call, how ironic, but it was about my future, and it sort of made me open my eyes. But then again, I haven't really thought about it much, so perhaps it's only opened one eye?

I was in an office, probably ten to twenty years from now, hard to tell, stress ages people, and I looked old. My secretary came in to tell me that someone named Isaac wanted to see me. I, or at least who I think was me, was much older and had a room that seemed to be organized by a very anal person, except the desk, the desk was very much cluttered and in disarray, filled with papers and the like. I told the secretary to send this, Isaac person, away, and she said that he was an old friend from many years ago. I couldn't remember him and was very busy, so I yelled something about me never having friends and said that he must be an imposter, to send him away. She stood confused for a while, so I told her that I was too busy for anyone and that I did not want to be disturbed EVER again. She left, and the dream ended right as the name Isaac made sense.

That's a bit disturbing, because I take great pride in the friends that I have. If my dream thinks that I won't care about them someday, then that's something to think about. So, I thought about it.

I've realized that lately I've been kind of a jerk, more than I am willing to admit to myself. I've been making little sarcastic, off-colored, on-the-square comments to people, taking little bites out of their self-esteem until it's no longer there. As fun as that sounds, I'd much rather be remembered as, "that quiet guy," than, "that bastard." So, I've decided to purposely change my attitude towards people...again. In fact, since I've decided this, I've noticed that I'm actually seeing more good in people, which is actually one of the things Dr. Shutz told me to do a long time ago – actually so have a lot of people – but I've never taken any of them seriously until now. Anyway, I'm hoping to improve upon this attitude of mine and put it to use by making it part of me. Hopefully, next time I have that dream, I'll jump up and run to meet Isaac.

Anyway, I haven't TOTALLY thought out this new attitude of mine, but I figure once I do, I'll write it down in my journal. But! I need to go pee, so I'll write about it later. Bye.

8
Jane

Today was devastating.

    As I was walking through the halls to class, I saw Isaac, which is unusual since he had work today and doesn't even go to community college. When I got closer to him, I saw that his eyes were red from crying and that he was standing against the wall, barely holding himself up. At this, I ran up to him to see what was the matter and before I could say anything, he grabbed me, yanked me through the halls, out the door, and to his car. I tried to ask what was wrong, but all he did was get into the car and motion for me to do the same, so I did. We drove in silence through the city, which I swear is larger than it was last time we all went out driving.

    "What the hell is going on? What's wrong ol' man?" I asked him.

    "Just...don't ask questions, you'll see...ok?" he said blankly.

    "What!? What's goin—"

    "OK!?" he screamed, and went silent.

    I sat quietly and noticed that we were heading downtown. At the time, I made only a small mental note, but I now realize why there were many ambulances, fire trucks, and police heading south towards the billowing black smoke. I didn't know where he was going until he turned into the hospital parking lot, driving like a maniac. That's when I knew it was bad.

Isaac has been through a lot in his life, much like I have (only he has handled it better), and finds it very difficult to show negative emotions, crying especially - I should learn from him.

He got out of the car quickly and told me to leave my stuff and to follow him. I did.

He started to run, and in the interest of not losing him, I started running too, all the while horrid thoughts poured through my head. He then took the stairs, and I knew it had gotten worse, and when he only went to the first floor, I knew it was awful.

Each floor of the hospital represents the condition of the patients on that floor; first floor is for critical patients and the fifteenth is for resting patients that are there basically to be taken care of. Everything in between is apparent, and I care not to go into them now or ever for it is an unimportant fact.

When I caught up to him, he looked at me with serious, deadpan eyes and said, "Frank and I are your best friends in the world and we WILL help you through this no matter what happens ok?"

I looked at him in disbelief and murmured an affirmative as he pointed to the door on his right. (*He begins to cry and a permanent tear is left on the page*)

When I walked into the room, my heart sank and I fell to my knees, because lying on the bed was Jane, my best friend in the whole world. She's always been more than a friend to me, despite our recent problems. She's helped me through more problems than Dr. Shutz or anyone else ever has or has even dreamed possible. If it weren't for her, I'd probably be dead on more than one occasion. She's more than Isaac and Frank could ever be. She's showed me love, admiration, attention, and got me started on a road that *I* screwed up. Even then she was the only one to come to see me almost every week for an entire year while I was in the institution, and the only reason she stopped is because the doctor told her to. Then, when I came out, she was one of the first ones to be happy to see me again, and now, here she is, lying on a hospital bed, covered with burns, cuts, several broken bones, and unstoppable internal bleeding. I can't continue...I'll finish this when I can put myself back together...*(He slowly puts His notebook down and watches her sleeping body, then looks to the others for hope, sees none, and begins to cry consistently for the second time in nearly eight years.)*

Today continues...unfortunately.

It's no better now. The doctor says surgery will not fix her internal damage. Apparently, a falling beam ruptured her kidney (and surrounding organs), and shattered half of her pelvic bone. Then, when she fell to the ground she hit her head on concrete, causing a concussion. And if that wasn't enough, a fire started and now she has third degree burns on thirty-five percent of her body, which the doctors tell me, is too much. So now, we wait on the 3rd floor wondering which will kill her first, bleeding to death, migration of bone fragments, a brain hemorrhage, or for her skin to suffocate and kill her?

I hate this! Why do these stupid things keep happening! Why can't this country rid the world of horribleness!? We tried it in 2002, in 2006, and now, why is it coming back so much, why can't we all just get along!

So, here I sit in this crappy old hospital, waiting for my Jane to wake up so that I can at least talk to her one last time.

We're all exhausted, confused, sad, angry, distant, and feel helpless.

Nothing's happening now, I'll write again when there is

Today is a bad dream - the worst...I wish...

I woke up and my first thought was, "Shit, what a messed up dream that was." But then I opened my eyes and the dream started anew. I scanned the room and saw that Isaac and Frank had fallen asleep in their chairs. The only light in the room came from under the door and from the Heart Monitor, which seemed to be reading steady and alive. I turned around and slipped open the curtains, only to notice that the sun was slowly dropping the last of its orange head below the horizon. It was late, and I didn't care, because I was not about to go anywhere anytime soon.

I sat quietly for a moment and decided that I should meditate and make peace with my inner Jane-self. I sat for nearly an hour in complete stillness just remembering the thousands of hours of phone time we spent together, the parties that we'd used to go to, and the quality time we all spent together. It was funny, we used to take turns being designated drivers, which I suppose was short lived because I only got to drive for several months before being admitted. I remember my sixteenth birthday party; all four of us got together and tried to drive to Vegas but we never made it, in fact, we didn't even get passed the city limits! I guess the prospect of ice cream and bowling outweighed the idea of loosing money and getting hookers. What the hell were we thinking, loosing money and getting hookers sounds like such a great idea right now! Hmph, so many stories told and untold, I think I might die just thinki

He looks up and sees Jane stirring in her bed. He instantly jumps up and runs to her side, dropping the notebook and pen to the ground. Her eyes begin to open and her hand grabs wildly at nothing. He instantly grasps her hand and holds it tightly to His chest. The doctors put Jane on very strong painkillers, so despite the burns across her face, she can feel nothing, including her hand in His,

171

but somehow she knows that someone has taken it and she knows who that someone is. After a few moments, she is able to open her eyes and right away confirms her feeling. She tries to say His name, but He tells her not to speak and to instead, listen.

"Thank you for everything," He says quietly, "I love you, and you have meant more to me than ANYONE in this world, you will not ever be forgotten." He smiles and turns to His two friends who are sleeping in the far corner, and attempts to wake them. He picks a gelatin cup off of Jane's uneaten lunch tray and throws it at Frank. Frank wakes and quickly notices Jane, so he shakes Isaac until he too is conscious. All three of them soon surround her bed quietly so that they can all be awake for her last hours.

Jane has been a life changer for all three of them, in fact. She was always positive and would never hurt a fly – unless of course that fly said that she was wrong.

She had helped them all, though, and now it was their turn to help her.

They all gather around closely and a smile creeps across her face. The three of them all look at each other serenely, each remembering the past and considering the future. A glint of sadness falls over their eyes, but they all smile nonetheless. All at once, they begin speaking, but the room is completely silent, for this group of friends does not need words to communicate.

All three of them take a chair without breaking their hold on her, then sit silently until they are all asleep again...

Today was the end.

I Won't Let Go

I hold you in my arms - You look up and try to speak,
"Save your energy,
You'll need it later,
Because I will not let you go!
Not now, not ever!
What will I do without you?

I need you!
YOU CAN'T DIE!
Please?
For me?
NO!
Open your eyes!
I will NOT let you Die HERE!
NOT LIKE THIS!
Please?
I'm so sorry
I could have done something,
It's my fault
Please…
Come back?
I still need you…"

I woke up this morning around two A.M. when the sound of the heart monitor stopped. I'm very good at ignoring things, but only when there is some sort of rhythm – there wasn't.

I looked instantly to the heart monitor and noticed that the little green dot was faltering spastically. I looked to Jane and saw that she was awake and gasping for air. I began to panic, but my better self took over and I calmed down quickly to assess the situation. I was able to get her attention, but she was unable to talk or breathe properly, so I hit the emergency call button. Within several seconds, two nurses came running in, then as fast as they ran in, they ran out, then appeared again with someone that seemed to be a tired doctor. Then, as fast as they had all come in, they were taking her to the ER for some unknown reason.

By the time all of this had happened the guys were awake, so we followed the nurse and increasing number of doctors to the ER, but were told to wait outside. The three of us toiled for what seemed like forever, but was only thirty minutes or so. The doctor came out and did not look at us for a long time, but we couldn't handle it and insisted on knowing what had happened.

"What's happened!?" we all asked at once.

The doctor snapped his gloves off slowly and glanced at each one of us, "Are any of you family?" asked the doctor.

"Her parents live very far away and won't be able to make it for another few days...we are her surrogate family, what's wrong?"

"Several of the bone fragments from her pelvis fracture, dislodged and traveled through the blood stream," he sighed, "the pieces got stuck in her lungs- we had to cut a lot open to get it out so she could breath..." he sighed again, "it's only a matter of time now before all of her organs start shutting down, there's just too much damage that the body can't deal with..." He trailed off and stepped out of the way in a gesture that told us we could go in to see her.

The majority of the anesthetics were beginning to wear off so she was mildly alert and recognized us almost right away. We all took turns saying our private good-byes, then came together, and said our group good-bye. I told her to, "put in a good word with God for me," we all laughed...only a bit.

For the next thirty minutes, we all sat around her and turned the nostalgia up full. We told stories that only we would think were funny and or interesting, like the time we all played hide n' go seek in the airport, or when we used the Kroger as a laser tag arena. We talked about the hundreds of dollars worth of movies we'd seen, and all of the matches I'd collected from all of the hoaky restaurants we ate at. Then came the part that we all dreaded. Because Jane has no immediate family in the area, it was up to us to discuss the funeral. We cried our eyes out during the twenty minutes that she explained what we were to do, and we promised to try as hard as possible to do everything she asked. She told us it was ok if we couldn't because of money or other lack of resources.

Her final wishes were that we each get a small urn with a bit of her ashes in each one, that way we could each have her at the same time without being jealous. ☺

We continued talking for another hour, and our conversation topics died out slowly, we held on to her tightly, so much so that if she was not on painkillers, the squeeze of our hands would outweigh the pain of what had happened.

It soon became very dark in the room and it was silent for what seemed like forever; the only light came from under the door and from the Heart Monitor's dying rhythm...

12/22 11:22 p.m.

I miss her.

I Missed You Today

> I missed you today
> But I guess that's ok
> I'll go on with life
> Through all of this strife
> I'm a magical man
> Please hold my hand
> I'll take you away
> I missed you today

Ack, I can't think of anything good or new, I'm going to bed.

12/23 2:40 p.m.

Today I was alive again.

It's been nearly a week since Jane died and I haven't been able to convince myself to write until today. We're all having trouble coping with what's happened, but because I'm the one with the mood disorder, I decided it best to write instead of bottling things up.

We've all stayed together in the apartment and haven't gone out much to do anything except to get food. Isaac worked without missing a day for nearly a year just so he could accumulate his sick time incase something like this happened – he gets paid to stay with us. Frank and I have nothing important to do, I couldn't care less about community college right now, so we're not in any immediate hurry to go anywhere; we stayed home as well.

For the last few days we haven't seen each other very often, my room has suddenly become an interesting place. When we all end up in the same room together – usually to pee or make food – it's quiet until one of us unexpectedly reminisces about the "good ol' days." Neither the TV nor the computer has been turned on since that horrible Tuesday morning, that's something to be damned proud of, or frightened of, either way it's something. It's times like these when I'm glad that I have the guys to take care of me, for without them I would surely be back in the institution by now.

Christmas came and went and none of us really noticed. It's an interesting holiday, I usually enjoy it thoroughly – so do they – but this year none of us enjoyed our present, and none of us could enjoy Christmas without Jane anyway. That's ok though, I didn't have any money or time to buy presents for anyone, I probably would have just made a card on the computer the night before. Oh well.

Anyway, despite the depression that's been floating over all our heads, we all seem to be doing ok. I mean, I haven't even broken anything yet, in fact, I've even cried a few more times...

Mm, I wonder what happens next, what WONDERFUL thing does the world have in store now!? Luckily, I got my grades up in ALL of my classes last week, so as far as other stress goes, I should be ok.

I'm tired and there's nothing to say right now, I'll write later when I can hold the pen without shaking...

12/28

Today I'm sad, angry, and depressed, but it's all good.

I'm so pissed now, just as I thought I would be, only worse! In the last week things seem to have hit the fan, first Jane dies, and the three of us were devastated of course, but now we have a funeral to plan and we keep getting into fights over what she wanted and what we can afford. Plus, to make matters worse, people keep calling us and reminding us of what happened – they all want us to help THEM through it. THEM!? What about us? Has no one even considered that perhaps her closest friends are going through just as much, if not more pain than everyone else is!? It's annoying and I'm sick of it ALREADY! Things were starting to settle down, and then I got a call from my mom. I tried to disguise my voice, but she knew it was me. In the interest of hope and in light of what happened last time, I attempted to calm down. She tried to console me but I was more unresponsive and rebellious to empathy, genuine or fake, so in the interest of not being an ass I remained quiet. It was successful to the point that I let her talk, but again, she seemed caring and asked me if I had anything to say, I said no, so she gave me a proverbial pat on the back and continued to talk. She mostly said that she was sorry for my loss and that she would do anything possible to help, I told her that we were ok, but any cooked food would be good, but that we still would not be good company. She said she would send food and that she understood, then hung-up. Now I'm confused about two things, Jane's death, and my mom.

I sulked for a while and thought about all of the things that I had to do for the funeral, and about all of the make up work that I'd have to do for school. I became depressed and angry again, but was too tired to really do anything about it, so instead I reminisced on my own. I became angrier still at the fact that we would not be able to do many of the things that we all used to do together. And if just the three of us did them, it would only bring back memories, and would not be the same. I was also saddened/angered about all of the ideas and things that we never did, and I continued to sulk – alone. When I was about to cry, the guys came home laughing hysterically and I didn't know why, but it was contagious and I soon laughed with them. It was a scary sight for anyone who could see us through the windows, because we were all laughing hysterically and had fallen onto the floor – it looked as though we were having seizures. When the laughing had finally died down, we all stood up, smiled, and were happy again. I didn't really care why we had laughed because the fact was, it made my day better, and I needed it.

We all sat down and apologized to each other for being jerks about everything, and we talked a bit more, mostly apologizing and putting closure to our whole situation. We planned the funeral finally, without arguing, and were not sad at all when we finished. Strangely, we all seemed satisfied and as happy as could be expected about planning a funeral, and were glad that we could all still be together and comfortable knowing that all was right with the world – sort of. The funeral is in one week, and I will write about it then…I need sleep, and I need time alone, I will not write until then…

New Year's Eve 8:32 p.m.

Yesterday was rare.

The funeral went well – as far as funerals go – it was very cliché. The rain poured down, painfully warm and dismal. Everyone Jane ever knew showed up in stark black outfits, holding on to umbrellas, memories, and missing large pieces of their hearts. The guys and I all had something to say, and so did her parents and two other friends of hers that we had never met before. It was all very sentimental and drab, and other than the attempted comedy of one person's speech, no one smiled. Understandable of course, seeing since the single most important person in my life as well as others' lives was no longer able to talk or play outside. The funeral's proceedings continued as planned, outside and in the rain, with the priest speaking Latin – as she was Catholic – and everyone listening intently as if they knew what was being said. I stood closest to the coffin to signify, mostly to myself, that I would always be there for her as she had been for me. I doubt seriously that anyone else noticed, but it meant something to me, and therefore was significant.

After the service, the three of us were horribly depressed, so in the spirit of continuing Jane's crusade against depression and discontent, we decided to take part in the best possible "Death Celebration" we could think of. The point of this celebration is to get drunk, then plastered, then horribly shit-faced in the remembrance of a passed soul; an Irish Wake.

We began our wake with a quick round of beers, then quickly graduated to whisky, brandy, and anything else with a high alcohol content and caramel coloring. We sulked quietly about the loss of Jane and what we would do without her. Our talk was mainly a repeat of early this week; it was neither productive nor interesting the second time around. I decided that we needed to get into the spirit of being drunk off our asses, so I went to the jukebox for some song. The Box was amazingly old, for it still used Compact Discs as opposed to ODN Chips. This, however, proved to be good, for on one of the CDs, I found the best Irish drinking song ever! TUBTHUMPING! The best song for the occasion in the world – as far as I have ever heard.

I programmed it to play three times consecutively, came back to the guys, and proceeded to dance as half-drunkenly and with as little rhythm as possible; I am white. By the end of its third playing we were all jumping around the room yelling (not singing) out the song, drinking heavily, and enjoying ourselves thoroughly.

Nearly four hours later, our simple whisky and brandy drinks had turned into massively complicated drinks consisting of more parts than I could count on two hands. By that time my muscle and nervous systems were about as fast and responsive as a rock, if not slower. Luckily though, at closing time Frank was only drunk and not shit-faced, so after scraping the two of us off the floor, he drove home so that we could collapse onto our floor without being "escorted" away by police. It was a fun ride home; I don't remember it.

It's late again or early, and I must sleep…or at least that's what THEY tell me! Like that'll be easy after being pumped full of enough coffee to write coherently! Of course, it is the next day, but STILL!!!…Hopefully something entertaining will happen tomorrow – bad drunken good day.

1/9/11 who knows, who cares!

9
The Labyrinth

Hope is gone...

I haven't written in a week. It's been one long, blurry day since Jane died and I don't remember much of what has happened between the funeral and now.

It's depressing really, how things seem to be going awfully good and then something horribly bad combats and destroys every bit of progress that I've made. I remember Doctor Shutz once telling me that I shouldn't let things bother me, but it's a bit difficult when those things are major events, like the death of my father and now the death of my best friend. I mean, it's just a little bit hard to ignore those things and stay positive and continue with my life. Of course, I suppose he meant with major things like this, I'm not supposed to dwell on them and not supposed to let them kill the motivating force in my life. But then, I haven't really let them do that, because I'm still alive, I'm still doing things, and I haven't committed suicide; I haven't even thought of that idea until just now. But I don't think I will continue to think of it either, for I have never really been one to end my own life due to uncontrollable circumstances.

Though, what am I to do now, that is, with my mind? As far as school and my social life are concerned, I suppose I will continue to live and do what I do now – survive. My grades are fine, no immediate problem there. I can put my social life on hold, people generally understand the need for silence and "grieving" as they call it, so I won't be bothered by people for now. My job is easily done; simple motions being repeated daily, no thought or emotion is put into that anymore – so long as there are no obnoxious customers. So then, what am I supposed to think about, how am supposed to get past this new mental obstacle? What do I need to do to accept these events and further fortify my conscious? I don't know yet. Perhaps it's not what I need to find out about this specific event, but more so what I need to finally find out about myself, and about the world. Maybe there is a much wider scope of things to see – a birds-eye-view perhaps?

Hmm…these are the questions that we ask ourselves on a constant and regular basis, are they not. I suppose only time and meditation will reveal the answers. Not so hopeless day?

1/15 12:25 p.m.

Metaphors and Similes.

I am the sad blind mouse who runs through the labyrinth, searching in vain for the delectable cheese. After years of searching, I have still never reached my goal. However, I continue trying, each time with some new piece of the maze engraved into my brain – my memory is improving – yet my sense of direction is deteriorating; a contradiction yes, but an absolute truth nonetheless, for I know what the path looks like, but I no longer know how or where to turn. Oh, what a wonderful game I play, not realizing that it is the same one each time, that is, until I find that familiar dead-end and have a chance to recognize the same colorful walls that I've passed millions of times before. Quite discouraging.

This maze is gigantic, complex, and seemingly endless. Complete with booby-traps, distractions (flashy lights, buttons, and sometimes other mice), and hundreds upon thousand of dead ends – each with their own effect on poor little old me. Though, this time is different, I can smell the cheese now, I feel as if I'm getting closer, but I cannot see what the cheese looks like, nor do I know what more I must endure to reach it. So, I press on, wanting help but receiving none. This time I am alone and I feel weak and tired, ready to quit. But I know that I am much stronger than I have ever been in my small life and I will continue to grow stronger as I go on. Therefore, I continue.

...I miss Doctor Shutz. He helped me. I miss Jane. She helped me as well. I fight for everything alone this time. But I know not what I am fighting for, though I know it is something great. It has to be...

1/20 10:12 p.m.

Today is difficult to label.

Isaac, Frank, Brittany, and I went out for dinner today after work and all that business garbage that takes place during the daytime. We went to Fuzzy Navel, a health food restaurant. I don't know who came up with the name, but the person obviously is a very odd and creative person. The food is good.

The conversation was light, all of us being either tired and burned-out from the day, or in deep meditation about what is supposed to happen next in our own lives (mostly mine). I ordered a BLT and soup – I haven't been very hungry lately –, Isaac and Frank ordered some frightening looking hamburgers, and Brittany had a salad and fruit – apparently she is on a diet, I don't know why, she has a beautiful body.

We talked about work and school and attempted to plan something for the weekend, but none of our schedules corresponded, so we quickly dumped that idea and moved on. Our conversation lacked the usual bounce and excitement typical of our normal conversations (those that date back to the teen age). It was rather depressing really. *I'm* rather depressed actually. I haven't wanted to do anything: eat, sleep, or even move. The guys had to practically drag me to the car; the only reason I went was to get away from the stagnant smell of the apartment (mostly created by the fact that I've not showered since that night of fun), and of course, to see Brittany. My hair is a mess, I'm unshaven, smelly, in dirty clothes, and don't even care. In fact, come to think of it, I don't believe I've ever come to this low a level, I at least clean myself when I'm depressed, now I'm betting I could be used as a chemical weapon in some unsuspecting country that we don't like. Or something like that. I...screw it, I've nothing more to write about because there's nothing more to say and I don't really care. I'm tired, burnt-out, depressed, dirty, lethargic, and every other word used to describe cows. Everything basically sucks and I feel pretty shitty all around. I've got nothing left. Dead, dying, blasé day.

1/27 9:44 p.m.

Finale.

Not much has happened recently, nothing of value or recognition anyway. I've not really concentrated on any one thing in particular; have just been going through the motions of each day. My weeks are one long day, consumed by little thought and many mindless tasks. I find myself bored quite often and don't see the excitement in things as I once did (worse then when I was in the hospital). I haven't written much because every time I think of something to write about, I either lose it or don't even have a point to begin with and end up rambling on about nothing. I've rambled on about nothing before, but it at least goes somewhere and ends up as something, now it's just words arranged on paper in a random, uninteresting manner.

I need to reflect right now, to organize the thoughts inside my head, and to find that positive energy flow again. Until then, which will be a while, I don't think I'll write…Good-bye for now.

2/12 1:01 a.m.

Trying something new.

I believe I'll go to church today, see how that works out. Wish me luck.

I've realized that I need people – ones that will help me realize myself – and that I'm really not alone, nor have I ever been.

I've also realized that, all my life I never really took responsibility for my own actions – let alone tried to correct those bad actions. In fact, I've tried to place everything on everyone else's shoulders and have blamed everyone else for my problems. My mom for example…it's not her fault entirely…she tried her best…and for that she is a much better parent than I have *ever* given credit for. As a child and a teen, I was completely bent on total independence, but I was immature about it – I never saw the big picture and was more self-centered than not. This worked because I learned many things through experience, and I became a somewhat stronger person because of it. Though, not as strong as I should have, for without people, I only learned from my limited scope of experiences (that I thought was everything in the world). Sure I figured things out by watching and learning from others' mistakes, though, I never bothered to listen to their thoughts and regrets about certain such things, thus I learned superficial answers, never anything deep or permanent. Thus, I ended up making the same mistakes as other people in order to experience them on my own, but didn't understand or know the consequences of those actions until it was too late. But I don't need to give examples of that.

Another thing is, I accept things readily, and that's good, but it's not. I accept things and then refuse to change that which is bad for me, because I am afraid of big change. A great example is my stay in the mental hospital (as usual). For the longest time I was content in the fact that I had beaten my mom and was residing in one of the state's finest facilities. I of course, played the game, and changed enough to get out, but I only scratched the surface, I never aspired to become better than just socially acceptable.

Well now it's different, this time I think I will grow and learn to be socially exceptional. Instead of "self-teaching" everything as I so expertly do, I should get involved in a community of people with hundreds of different problems. I should take the time to listen to them, to listen to how they sort out their troubles, to listen to how they still go through those problems, yet persevere despite it all. Maybe then I'll make more progress then I ever have before.

My friends have helped me, of course, but they are also at the beginning of their lives, dealing with their own problems and obstacles. It's unfair to them for me to want so much of their attention, to burden them with every little issue of mine. No, I will still love them, but not in a nagging, whining, troublesome way, but in a caring, real friend sort of way – it's time for me to be there for them.

Instead, I think that I will find other people, people that don't require deep relationships and one hundred percent attention. Maybe these people (perhaps a church community) will be ones that I can bounce ideas off of, learn from, and listen to, without the obligations associated with the relationships I have now. I know this sounds superficial, but I think that it's exactly what I need, and if I'm wrong about how to go about this kind of help, then I suppose I will receive none. But perhaps some of the people I will meet today will also be looking for the same thing that I'm looking for...perhaps I will find someone, or something that will finally fill in that last piece of my puzzle.

I don't know, I'm scared, but it's an anxious exciting scared, so I allow it and I enjoy it. In fact, from this day, I no longer fear social situations, I'm ready to go out there and meet new people and try new things. I'm ready for a change...again...

Facing Fear

I start to walk,
I hear a noise
I Stop.
Silence –
I Start again,
I see a shadow
I turn around
Nothing is there
I continue.
I suddenly turn around!
I see him!
Fear!
He stalks me!
I look into his eyes and laugh –
He looks into my eyes and laughs –
I am confused
I take a step forward,
He disappears
I have finally won

Haha! I won! Look at that! I await the day jubilantly!

3/12 8:04 a.m.

10
Words of Wisdom

Today was short, but I have much to say.

WOW! I haven't written in like…four months almost! A LOT has been going on lately. Community college is over, my friends still love me, and I'm looking at life with a whole new attitude. Details below:

First off, I passed my final exams of last year, which is good, but I nearly killed myself in the process. Studying is hard, especially since I never felt it necessary to study in middle or high school, and now that I do, my habits are a bit strange. But oh well, whatever works. It's funny, in the interest of taking a lot of notes quickly I've learned to write with my right-hand as well as with my left. That way, when one gets cramped I can just switch it over to the other one and so on. Although, my right-handed writing is considerably less readable, it still works for me, so shut up. Now, I have enough credits to equal my last year in high school because I took and passed a few simple summer school classes and got my GED. So, I think I'll work for another school year's worth of time, save up some money, and go to college. I don't know what I'll major in, but I know it'll be fun because I'll learn and do things and learn to do things.

Which reminds me, I'm working at the Monster Movie Theater, it pays eighteen dollars an hour with my Managerial position. So I've been living pretty well seeing since I share the rent and bills, and I don't eat much or do much by myself. Well, except when I have a girlfriend.

Speaking of that, I just ended a two-month relationship. I loved that kid, we did lots of fun things together, and I think we were connecting really well, I thought we had a future together, but she didn't share that feeling. I guess I kind of freaked her out when I told her that I loved her, things got awkward for her from there and she left me. Almost right away she found someone else too, I made a big ass of myself at the music store she works at when I found out her co-worker was the new guy. I probably shouldn't have said some of the things I said, but she shouldn't have said some of the things that she said either. I guess we both kind of flipped out and got jealous and all that other break-up anger stuff. But, she doesn't want to talk to me and I'm afraid to talk to her, so I guess I'll never get a chance to apologize in person. And I know she'll never pick up the phone if I call...so that's the end of that love story.

Lately, I've thought a lot about some of my past relationships. It seems that, while I profess to people that I don't enjoy relationships and all the stress and confusion and mind games that come with, I am in fact, very much dependant on a girlfriend. I always seem to *think* that I love that person, so I smother them to the greatest extent of smothering, or I am completely distant from that person because I don't know what I really want. I fear love, but I want it, so I constantly look for it. I suppose that's normal though, because everyone wants love of some kind or another. Love, what a strange thing, I've been learning quite a bit about love and people and loving people lately. I've also been reading a lot of old letters from my dad and from other people that used to help me. My own entries even tell me that I'm doing things wrong. Apparently, I used to be a rather cold person. I have a frighteningly serious disposition most of the time, and that scares people away. Also, I am sometimes very self-centered, I suppose that's what being cold is?

Oh well though...The guys and I weren't hanging out much anyway, especially since I was always staying at her house instead. So now, I have a chance to be with them, hang out all hours of the night, and do stupid things again, right? OH! Frank's birthday is coming up soon too! That means we're all going to go hunting for whatever looks tasty, so that will be great fun, I haven't used my rifle in a LONG time. Hmm, if only she could be there with us, she liked to hunt...

ANYWAY! Umm...oh ah! Whelp, it's getting a bit late, so I'm going to go have an orange and go to bed. Or stay up and read something insightful. I'll explain my new attitude later. Until then...

7/1 10:48 p.m.

My new attitude.

I decided to start going to church after Jane died because I realized that no matter how hard I could try to take care of myself, I really couldn't do it after all. The first time I went, I don't think the message was for me, but the man who spoke it was.

While I was walking out, he was at the door greeting people and right away noticed that I was new. In his sermon, he had explained that he majored in psychology as well as theology – an interesting an intelligent choice if you ask me. As he talked to me this became extremely evident, for he was already beginning to figure me out from the few answers, or lack thereof, that I had given him. It scared me at first so I was quiet, but that gave him a chance to talk and explain to me why logicalizing everything in the Bible is bad. He even quoted scripture where it says something about using your heart instead of your mind (I sadly don't remember it's been so long now). So, I continued to talk to him and he said that he would take me to workout (he thought I was a wrestler because of my "body type") and if I had questions or was interested in the Bible or just wanted to talk to me, he would listen etc. I took him up on his offer, so now whenever we aren't busy we work out together, talk about things: Bible, women, life. We don't see each other as often anymore though because I only go to church on Saturdays and he usually is the youth pastor, but he showed me something about people and myself that I'll probably never forget no matter how hard I try – not that I'd want to.

Because of him – and others –, I've decided that whatever petty insecurities and "issues" I had in the past are now all very dumb, and that I'm over them for good this time. Although, you get a lot of attention and pity from people when you're messed up in the head, I figure I can get attention other ways, and be totally stable at the SAME TIME! Especially since I resist most of that sympathy attention anyway. That's basically why people hang on to their problems anyway isn't it?

I mean, there shouldn't really be any other reason why you can't get over something is there? Things happen, it might scar you, but eventually scars heal too, and if you hold on to something horrible in your past, then you're only going to screw yourself over in the future. The only reason to hold on to the past is so that you can bring it up to someone one day and they can feel whatever emotion they want for you, but the point is, you're getting attention for it. This is what I've done for the longest time. I'm not saying it's necessarily bad if you only do it a little bit, but if you let it effect you're whole life (like hating the world, hating God, not trusting people, etc.) or anything else negative that comes out of it, then you're the one that's losing. And if you're a lonely freak with absolutely NO ONE to talk to, then by all means, screw yourself over, but if you have friends and family that care about you, you sure as hell better start fixing yourself or getting help, because it's not only ruining your life, but it's affecting the people around you as well.

One of the only ways to do that is by forgiving, forgetting, moving on, and thinking positively about the events in your life. Lots of people always look at the worst part of a situation, and then do something stupid because the world isn't nice to them! You can't expect the world to just be nice to you, you have to try just as hard if not harder than it to get something good. Just because the world throws a huge curve ball of junk at you doesn't mean you have to curl up in a ball, start rocking, and give up. I've seen too many people give up on the world then threaten to commit suicide because they can't take it. My first reaction is to tell them to go ahead with it because it's their life and they're taking up space. But now, I see that it makes for much better conversation and a more interesting day if I sit down and talk with that person and try to tell them not to turn out like me, and instead, to have fun and do stupid things because it's cool and often times taste good.

So ah, anyway, sorry, I went off on a tangent, so where was I...hold on...Anyway, like I've said before, I'm going to grow up and stop being a wimp that can't even handle something bad in my life every once in a while.

Umm, I think I'm done, I'm sure I'll think of more, but you all get the idea...

Just look at the bright side of everything, deal with life as it comes to you, don't dwell on the past, don't lie to your friends, and if you MUST have sex PLEASE wear a condom. Good day!

7/2 12:35 p.m.

What next?

It seems now that I have come to a point in my life where I do not know what to do next, again.

Firstly, I would like to continue saving up money, for I now have about twenty thousand dollars or more, with interest and all of that other junk; I think I'll call the bank after I finish writing this entry. Anyway, I would much like to go to college so that I can do something profound with my life, so far I've thought of teaching because it would fit my personality quite well. Many people don't take me seriously because teaching is not considered a very honorable job, but for the fact that I would be passing my large amounts of trivial knowledge on to the future generations, is honorable to me.

In all seriousness though, it fits my personality because: my ego will allow me to enjoy taking control of a group of lesser people (in a nice way), I do not generally care what people think of me anymore so I can look like as much an idiot as possible, I'm very good at explaining things in several different ways, and can also learn easily myself. Plus, I have lots of neat stories to tell! Of course, now the only problem is, what subject do I teach? For that I have absolutely no idea, a lot of people have said Philosophy because I always have something to say about everything or everything to say about something, but I think the class is mostly an annoying history lesson, I really don't know, either way I'd like to take it. Other than that though, perhaps I could teach English or science, or astronomy, or something related to Star Trek, I've always loved Star Trek. Or maybe pop-culture! I could teach about MY era, the hundreds! Who knows, I don't. I suppose I'll be "undeclared subject" or whatever it is they call it when you want to be a teacher but don't know what to teach.

Secondly, I would much like to get in touch with my dad's last wife, I want to talk to her and learn more about him, see what he was like towards the end. In fact, I would much like to get in touch with the remainder of my entire family, for I've recently decided that family is not so bad after all and in fact, they can be fun and good for your health. I've decided this because my mom and I have been getting along lately, so much so that we've gone to dinner together and other public places without fighting and have actually started to reconcile our differences; we're both happy about it, in a strange sort of way. So I think I will go on a road trip around the vast country we call America with Isaac and Frank (if I can convince them to leave the computer), so that I can find my "roots" and learn from them. This seems important to me suddenly, and that is probably a good thing.

Thirdly, I would like to further my religion for several reasons. One, what would it hurt to learn a little bit about God and his morals, they are generally good and if nothing else, funny. In fact, I'm willing to bet that God and I have a lot in common, in a less omnipotent way that is. I mean, he's a moody person, very secure in his superiority but it doesn't take much for him to get pissed off and hurt someone. Also, he wants to teach people, SO DO I! See we're getting along already, I'm sure there's more things, but Pastor Yossarian (My workout buddy) says that when I talk like this it borders on blasphemy, so I should probably stop – ah right! Besides, why not be religious and get saved? If I do learn to believe these magical Bible things truly with my heart, I'll get baptized and I'll go to heaven. If there is no God, I will have led a good life and gotten a free public bath out of the deal. Anyway though, God may be crazy, but so am I and so is everyone else, so why not just join the crowd that can't be beaten and see what it's really all about? I'm still a "wandering Christian," but it's actually not so bad as I thought. I'm always wondering where my part in "THE PLAN" is and why I need God, but I'm sure that it will all be revealed subtly, like a brick to the head.

In the meantime, I suppose I will just work my butt off ordering teenagers around at the movie theater, thus teaching them responsibility and also giving me something to do, for working at a movie theater is a joke. I'm hungry hold on…

Mmm, dehydrated cereal, just add milk! What will they think of next? That reminds me! It seems that recently things in the world have been getting better. For example, the Eurasian problem has taken a turn for the better, the tensions of war have somewhat diminished so that they are no longer a daily threat to the world, although there is still a threat nonetheless, just smaller. Also, it seems that the government finally decided to retake its fallen territory and has issued a large number of new reforms that, within many years, could help to save this country from itself. Our government has also increased the education budget, as well as enforcement and several other suffering areas. Perhaps these things will help crime and ignorance…or perhaps they will all stay the same. No one is to know until it is over and done with and the numbers are collected. Finally, it seems that everything has come full circle, for I am better, the world is better, and everything is in its right place. Now the only thing left to fix is TV, and everyone else. ☺

I have much more to say, but I need a break from writing, my hand is cramped. Bye for now.

7/3 2:30 p.m.

I few poems that I've written that express the new me better than an entire entry can.

Empathy

The ability to feel you
The ability to know you

The ability to understand you
The ability to be you

It was once something,
That I had none of
It is now something,
That I am so sure of.
I know myself,
Who cares.
I almost know you,
Who cares.
I want to know you,
But can't?
Can I?
When you don't know me,
Not a thing, nothing; know.
Yes. To know, to feel, to be, to see.

These things I want,
Who cares?
Why? I don't; no.
But I do, need more
Empathy…
These things I've had not
This thing I have now
I care.

Mental Clarity

I stare off into space
Not confused
Not lost
But completely aware.
Of the world
Of myself

Of everything,
It's all so clear
It all fits together,
So simply
Yet so complicated at first
It took me hundreds of years
To reach this level,
This level of Mental Clarity

The world is an interlacing,
Of positive and negative energy
Sometimes we find good
Sometimes bad
Often a mix,
But the key is
To find the positive
And ride its waves,
This task is difficult
You must concentrate
You must want it
You must need it
And most of all,
You must be open to all things
Every side of the circle
Each aspect of the universe,
Only then
Can you begin *your* journey
Your journey beyond these barriers,
For your mind is limitless
As are you

So take this first step
With me,
We can accomplish anything
And overcome all obstacles,

To reach complete, and total
Mental Clarity

I especially liked these two, I think I'll write one or two more, but not right now, I have a few things to do before I go to bed, thoughtful week.

7/3 11:35 p.m.

Getting out of the car, He turns to His friends who remain in the car, "Aren't you guys going to come in with me?"

Isaac responds, "Living with you is a trip enough, we don't need to see an entire room filled with crazy people, you go ahead and do whatever it is you need to do on your own, we'll just hang out here."

"Ok," He says, then turns, walks across the parking lot and into the hospital, where He immediately recognizes the old front-desk nurse. She too recognizes Him, and looks questioningly at Him. "Don't worry, I'm a visitor today, I just wanted to test something on my own," He says to reassure her.

"Oh? And what's that," she says genuinely interested.

"Well, as you know, I lived here for a long period of time and I've only just recently let go of my old self. I wanted to come back to make sure I'm ready to move on, to be certain that everything is in the past, and what better way to do that than to actually visit the place it all sort of started?"

"Well I don't know what exactly you're expecting to find or what it will prove, but I suppose it would be okay with the doctor if I let you look around for a while."

"Thank you, Hilda."

"Anytime, honey," she winks at Him, makes Him sign in, gives Him a visitor badge, and returns to her work.

Roaming around, He is filled with intense feelings of nostalgia and excitement as He touches old game boards and the chairs that are scattered throughout the game room. The hospital is quiet because it is group therapy time. He wanders through the halls carrying His journal with Him. He stops when He sees the spot on the wall where He used to sit and rock and think each day. The worn paint and indent in the wall still have not been repaired. He stares for a moment, and suddenly sits in the spot – His back still fitting perfectly in the indentation –, opens His journal, pauses for a moment to think, and finally writes:

I feel less fearful of the world today.

And that is why this will probably be my last entry *ever*. For about a year now, I have written in my journal about every major thought that I have had about many things (never all things), and I have rationalized, justified, and calmed myself nearly every time, consistently and logically. I have learned a great many things throughout my life, I have experienced just as many, and I now no longer find it necessary to write everything down in order to keep myself in control. But in order to put closure to what has played an important part in life, I will continue writing for as long as my mind and or my hand will let me.

Also, poetically and ironically, I am at the moment writing from my old spot in the corner in the mental hospital. I didn't expect this to be my last entry, but when I came here, it felt so full circle that I decided I was ready to take my last step; to move on completely. I have nothing more to say about the hospital or the people in it, other than I'm glad to see them all one more time (though I'm disappointed that they are all still here) before I move on and forget this chapter of my life completely. I had originally intended to give Doctor Shutz my journal, but I can't find him and I don't think he would be able to use it, so instead I will do something else with it; I haven't decided what though. So, I will end my journal here in the hospital where it began and everything will be in its right place.

It seems that life, in the most complex way possible, is very simple, and in fact, can be summarized into probably less than two hundred pages of nonsensical, incoherent babbling. This alone, can even be broken up into smaller, easier to understand parts, for example, happiness (I have a story about that which I will stick in the end of this entry) and other emotions. These emotions are what rule our lives, whether it is how many we have, or how many we don't have, it's how we use them that makes the difference. Many people go through life living naïvely and happy for no apparent reason at all. I once criticized people like this because I found that their minds were empty and lacked substance. Then, there are people that live life angry at everything, and do not ever learn or explore anything other than what immediately surrounds them. I also criticized them, for they experience nothing. Though, after thinking about all of the different people that I have criticized over time, I came to realize that in one way or another, I am just like all of them in at least one aspect or another. So in essence, I am criticizing myself as well. Along with this thought, I decided that perhaps the naïve person is very much more intelligent than I am, because he or she *chooses* to be that way. Besides, what is so wrong about being naïve, at least you are sheltered from the horrors of reality. Then, I thought about the angry person that sees no good, perhaps in a sad sort of way, this person is preventing himself from ever getting hurt by anything or anybody. Then there are the infinite combinations of people with ideas and behaviors that I might never understand, and I look at them and realize, to each their own, for whatever works for them should work for me as well. For the fact that I cannot change people, I should not ever complain that they are different, because, believe it or not, some people don't like me either.

Love. It is something that neither I nor anyone else will ever fully understand. The Bible explains it best when it says, "Love is patient, love is kind. It does not envy, it does not boast, it is not proud. It is not rude, it is not self-seeking, it is not easily angered, it keeps no record of wrongs. Love does not delight in evil but rejoices with the truth. It always protects, always trusts, always hopes, always perseveres. 1 Corinthians 13:4-7." When I read that, it summed up everything I've always believed in or have tried to say about love, because it is true and is not a mushy warm feeling, but is action. With that definition I found that I truly love many more people than I thought or thought possible, but also found that there are plenty of people that I need to learn to love more. For I love my friends, Isaac and Frank, Jane, and Brittany; they've been with me from the beginning to the end and throughout it all despite their physical presence. I also love my mom, for I never thought it possible, but somewhere in me, I always have and always will, but again, could definitely have loved her a lot better than I did or do now. Also, I need to stop analyzing so much. Many people at church say that I think too much or that I have, "too much head knowledge," and that I'm too smart for my own good and for God's good. I think too much, and I am beginning to agree. I lack compassion and I lack that which *starts* deep relationships. I am very lucky to have Frank and Isaac, and the reason it works between us, is because we are guys and don't need constant hugs and affirmations of each other's love. Love it seems, is the single most important thing in the world to many people in at least one part of their life and in at least one way or another. Without love, none of us would really truly exist in the way that we are supposed to. Without love, we would be worse animals than we are now, for love is what makes us all human, it is the one thing that separates us from the beast and from any alien species that might ever land on this sorry planet. Love, is what makes good people.

Life. Life is simply complex and I love it because it is everything and more. Many people believe in a lot of different meanings to life: Money, sex, divine truth, work, having fun, and to live to die. Truthfully, all of those are wrong and all of those are right, for life is anything that you want it to be because if you do not have your own reason to live, then there is seriously no reason for you to live. Suicidal people used to ask me why they should live and what the point to life was. I would tell them that there was no point to life, that there is no reason for us all to be here on a gigantic spot in the middle of the Universe, and they would get mad at me for saying so. I would then explain to them that it is not my place to tell them what to live for, because despite the fact that I knew the person, I did not know what the person wanted in their life. Most of the time, my suicidal friends were looking for attention, as is everyone, and they never actually would do anything. My point is though, it is not my place, nor anyone else's, to tell you why you should live. It is up to you to find where you fit in the world, the only thing that you MUST do, is have as much fun as you possibly can. For this is what will create good people and healthy lives.

Do whatever means something to you. Think of your life, and think of what you would regret missing if you died tomorrow, really think about it and then go do as much of it as you possibly can. What's important is relative, do what's important to you no matter what others think but try not to put them down in the process. Whatever makes you happy is all you're really living for, so do it as much and as often as possible and is healthy. If you are stuck doing something you hate, stop, no matter what the consequence, including people, it might hurt them, but truthfully, if they want you to suffer in order to keep them happy, they aren't the types of people worth keeping happy. Besides, they'll understand sooner or later. If you hate yourself, change yourself. Change will be hard as hell to do, and I recommend finding someone who can help you through it; a good friend if you can find one or a therapist with a cluttered office. When you have changed enough to like yourself and your life, it will all be worth it. To live is to change, and if you don't change anything, you are not alive. "If you do not want to be forgotten as soon as your are dead, either do something worth writing, or write something worth reading." That is the best quote in the world.

Criticize everything mentally and come up with your own opinions on everything so you can make small talk and so you have confidence. I am sick of people buying into one huge opinion and one huge viewpoint of the world. Do things you'll regret, otherwise you haven't lived, but don't do something too stupid, because you'll live in a prison – mental and physical alike. Be whatever you want to be, you will find you are whoever you think you are and it doesn't matter what anyone else thinks because it's not their life. Whatever is real to you is real, period. If you saw it, it was there, maybe not for everyone, but for you it was.

You should never: Kill nice people, draw conclusions before you know the entire situation, be an asshole, disrespect people regardless of their respecting you, tell little girls they're fat, or burp loudly in public.

Parenting. I do not think that I will want to be a parent for a long long time to come, in fact, I think I'll wait until I'm retired or dead. I have been observing people, and always will observe people, and I have found that in order to raise another human, you must always be on your toes, always thinking, always anticipating, and always being randomly consistent. A child is not a toy no matter how cute and plastic he or she looks. A child's mind is not a computer, and cannot be fixed by pushing buttons, but can be ruined by an annoying virus, proverbial or real. A child must be taught responsibility with trust and encouragement, taught lessons through word of mouth and experience, and taught discipline with a firm hand and by example. And then it gets harder, because the child gets older; we call these the teen years. After that, it is up to what he's learned, his upbringing, his parents love for one another and for him, it's up to his large amount of limited freedom, and it's up to his friends to save him from those years, the world, and himself. Then it gets easier for the parent and harder for him; we call this college. He unlearns, relearns, and learns everything again for the first time. The parents wait, smile, understand, and he is reborn with facial hair, strange clothes, and a vegetarian attitude (if you're lucky). Love him...no matter what. Or, there is the space-saver way. Adopt instead. There are too many people in the world already that are neglected. Take care of one of them instead of making your own, it just seems like a waste, and it saves money on baby supplies if the child is already old enough to pee in a toilet. Also, it makes for a more interesting marriage when you have a kid that understands the facts of life and can play outside for the time being.

Health. Health is important, it belongs with love, but you can touch it, so it is separate. Clean yourself regularly, behind your ears, in your mouth, and under your arms. Shave when and where needed, for hair is generally disgusting unless you know how to trim it properly and or comb it nicely, and you probably don't. Exercise regularly, it will make you feel better physically and mentally, people will notice, and your life will feel better. Exercise is not always weight-lifting, it is reading, it is running, it is getting up off of the couch, stretching, moving more than usual, and thinking. These things will save you. Health is important, never claim apathy, ignorance, or laziness, it is not good for your health.

God. God exists and he does so because he wants to. Everyone needs God in one way or another, whether for emotional or mental support, to keep them alive, as a friend, as a reminder of all that is good and big in the world, or as a person to shun, doubt, and ignore. Despite the fact that God has created wars, he is cool, because without him and without those wars, the world would be boring and would be ruled by Romans. Romans are cool, but are eccentric and probably too stupid to ever find America, plus, they defecate publicly and in groups of twelve with no separation between each person –

Columbus was Roman Catholic. Also, without religion, there would be no tax exempt buildings to be friendly in, the world would be worse off than it is now, and many aimless, stupid people in the world, would not ever be able to find their way through the darkness and would forever be isolated. However good this might be, the suppressing of sheep, we would have no one to compare ourselves to and it would be unfair in general to those who lock themselves away. Luckily, these people find religion. Without religion there would be no end times, thus there would be nothing for millions of Bible Scholars to do with themselves and no one would really know why they were living (Thus heaven). Without God, more bad things would happen than good things because human nature dictates that we all want a can of worms to open, and what good would a million worms do us? Without God, many African tribes would not know what White People are – We are Gods or Satan depending on the region. Without God, many people would go to bed every night, without praying. Without God, none of us would be here. And without God, we would all kill animals when we stepped on bugs and the Bible would never stop being written. God how annoying *that* would be.

I will now write the Key to Happiness to the person who finds this notebook, for I have decided to lose it in a large crowd of people, hoping that it will be put to use or will be burned in order to warm a homeless family.

Imagine if you will, a somewhat large object floating through space. Now keep in mind that in space, there is absolutely no friction, therefore, this object will continue to float through space at the exact same speed and direction as it started, until another force acts upon the object (normally gravity of planets and other related spatial bodies). This other force will cause the object to lose energy and slow down – never stopping – but, when it exits the orbit or perimeter of this object's force, it will gain energy and continue on through space, perhaps in a different direction and with even more energy than it started with. This cycle will repeat itself for many trillions of years until either the universe itself is destroyed, or for some odd reason, the object is destroyed.

Now let me explain this in terms of life, incase you can't quite find the connection.

You are the object, the initial force that sends you on this journey is not being born, but it is the thing that makes you happy. This force cannot be alterable, and must be created from within (if it is an outside source, the source must be with you throughout your entire life and should not change – perhaps God?). Now, the other forces (such as relationships, work, school, mood swings etc.) will cause you to lose your energy/happiness. In the case of love, you will be stuck in an orbit so-to-speak, but even orbits decay and the object continues floating (much like MOST love stories). However, if you can retain the original energy from the very first force, you can continue a healthy, happy, joy filled life no matter what.

This here, is what I believe to be the key to life (not meaning). All you need is your ONE thing (or many things if you like) that makes you happy, whether it is the memory of family, your talents, abilities, confidence, etc. If you find this ONE thing to hold on to and focus on, your life will be much better, but only if you don't cover that thing with worries and other garbage that's not important. Because, no matter what you get stuck on (death of family/friends or otherwise lesser or greater depressors), you can still gain that energy back, all you need is that force (not the Star Wars force). All too often people become preoccupied with things that aren't important. Know yourself and worry about yourself FIRST, then take care of others that are in need, and make sure you guard yourself from those things that damage you. Avoid stress and self-help books where possible, and if you can't, find a way to flush those things out of your mind, whether it is venting or other. Over all, in space, much as in life, nothing can stop you from doing anything but your own lack of motivation, your own inability to adapt to a situation/rules, and worrying. Sometimes though, circumstance can put you on hold/in orbit I understand, but those things are temporary and you can work around them if you care to.

So I say to all of you people that think your lives suck and you hate everyone because your dog beats you, your mom thinks you're a devil child, your TEACHERS are the ones giving you bad grades, and your boyfriend or girlfriend doesn't *really* love you and instead just wants sex. Stand up to your dog, respect your parents MORE than you already do (tell them you love them and blow their minds), start shutting up in class and doing the work, and stop having middle school relationships. This is to myself as much as to everyone else because I am aware that I have just as many faults as everyone else does.

Also, there are many ways to fix all of your small problems if you really care to. For example, if you want attention, color your hair, it's a sure-fire way to get all the love you want. If you have no friends, be loud. Don't know what to do with your life? Set lots of large goals then throw in mini-goals on the side. If you don't like people, join the group of people that doesn't like people and you'll suddenly have people you like and your cause will be lost among disgruntled friends. If you are an outcast, start your own group, there are always more outcasts that will join you, you will no longer be an outcast, and will in fact, fit somewhere. If you have no self-esteem, grow some or buy some. If you have too much self-esteem, piss off someone bigger than you, or get an arrogant friend, either way you'll be humbled and or bloodied – both work well. If you don't know yourself, ask people that you're around to notice things about you and to be blatantly truthful. Don't understand the world, question everything. Hate the world, change it, or change yourself. As for other things, stop CREATING your own problems, because if you don't have a clearly defined mental illness, you have no reason to act like you do unless it's purely in the name of fun.

So I conclude by saying that, despite the fact that we are all crazy humans, we must live together without killing one another, and that no matter how hard life gets, if you are strong, you must remain calm, look to your problems, and work them out logically and with heart. For this is the only way to beat the world and live in it too, because if you don't play your cards right, you will end up just like me, only worse…Good life, good day, good thoughts, and good karma, for these things will save us all…

Controlled Burn

As the building burns warm
Smoke fills the room
Through all the chaos
A pianist does play,
His song is not dead
But of triumph and joy,
The masterpiece is his
While the building burns hot
By an uncaring flame
The musician's song grows

Suddenly - no warning
Framework does crack
Walls fall flat
Wood snaps grotesquely
Like bones being crushed
But the man still plays

Michael Lee

— For he will not stop
The climax is nearing
So the man plays more,

High notes are screaming!
Low notes do roar!
His fingers pound wildly!
This sound is so rare!
As the building falls down
    — Beams all around
Inferno of life
    — Is no longer strife
His song is near ending!
For he plays with great passion!
He hits the last chord!
Then holds it forever!
And the building's no more…

        7/4 Anytime is good for me.

And with that, He closes His notebook and walks outside to meet His friends. Before reaching the pavement, He stops to look upon the familiar building with an expression of joyous finality and a hint of de ja vu. At the same triumphant moment, an old, wise, graying man, comes out of the entrance and stands staring at his favorite patient with proud, loving eyes, wondering what waits for Him in the coming years. Suddenly, the younger man drops His notebook, and runs to His favorite Doctor to embrace him in much the same way that He would His own father. They both look into each other's eyes and quietly say good-bye for the last time.

As the four of them speed through town, there is an Independence Day Parade marching down Main Street. He sees this crowd, and with suddenness and excitement, opens the window and rips all of the electric and paper sheets from the binding of His notebook and throws them into the crowd. Each page flies through the air, performing a ballet all its own, then lands peacefully on the hearts, minds, and souls of the people outside.

Epilogue

Twenty years later, 2031, He is the owner of a large genetic research compound, having written His thesis on an unorthodox cloning technique. He also teaches English to under privileged kids and is somehow able to incorporate His life into the teachings of diction and other such nonsensical literary terms. His wife, an Elementary School teacher that He met in college, is now pregnant with a young boy whose name will be Lee. His mom, who has held on through the years, battling cancer and other annoying ailments of the sort, still nags at Him, but in a loving way, for they finally have the relationship that a mother has with her son while He's still in the womb – only with two-way conversations.

Isaac and Frank come over whenever they can to hang-out and, depending on the mood, talk about "the good ol' days," when they still had all of their hair, had simple jobs, no wives, and all of the freedom they could ever want. Though, when they talk to each other, any eavesdropper could not follow, because their words are backed with history so thick and so deep, that often times even they have trouble understanding what's being said, if there are indeed words being said at all. Isaac is now a full time writer with a contract from a well-known publisher, and Frank is now an upper-middle-class private accountant, with a paycheck that weighs over a pound. Together, the three of them and their families are one entity, because they all have the most important thing in common, Love.

About the Author

Michael Lee (Michael Higdon) is a senior studying language arts and social sciences. Entranced with the ideas of personality and ego, he wrote *Journal of a Mental Patient* as well as essays and articles for his underground newspaper. These writings discuss such issues as egoism/objectivism (inspired by Ayn Rand), the plight of society as caused by technology, hope for the future that lies in the enlightened individual, why TV is the devil, and other such bullocks.

Born in Las Vegas, Nevada, Michael lives a most interesting life as he constantly seeks all of life's experiences. Before the age of eighteen, he traveled the entire country and had almost unlimited freedom; he uses these experiences to enrich his writing.

www.ingramcontent.com/pod-product-compliance
Lightning Source LLC
Chambersburg PA
CBHW030310290526
45785CB00001B/293